Denominations

Researched and written by

James Jobe

While every precaution has been taken in the preparation of this book, the publisher assumes no responsibility for errors or omissions, or for damages resulting from the use of the information contained herein.

DENOMINATIONS

First edition. August 21, 2024.

ISBN: 979-8227942395

Written by Marvin McKenzie and James Jobe.

Table of Contents

Introduction

MY MOTIVATION FOR COMPILING this study is solely for informing Independent Baptists and other Bible believers what is taught and believed by the religious groups covered. I have no personal bias, nor did I begin with any preconceived negative feelings against any religious group.

All research was performed by me personally, originally in 2007, and reviewed and revised in 2018 and 2023. As much as possible the quotes are from denominational sources first, and outside sources second. I used books and websites that were easily available. All conclusions are my own personal beliefs based on the research that I performed. No Church or other religious institution is responsible for these conclusions.

I trust that this study will be a blessing to all Bible believers and help us to have compassion for all those who are deceived by the false doctrines taught by most of the religious groups covered.

James Jobe

James Jobe

P.O. Box 688

Tonasket, WA 98855

(509)429-5528

kjbprechur@gmail.com

Used by permission

"Here are all the lessons and other necessary pages. You have my permission to publish them as you see fit. I hope and pray that my feeble efforts at research will be a blessing to someone."

Foreward

IT HAS BEEN MY PLEASURE to have served as a brother and fellow preacher of the gospel with Pastor James Jobe for – well – the better part of 40 years. Pastor Jobe has done a great service to his brethren in the Baptist churches community. When I discovered this work I was thrilled to have the opportunity to publish it for a broader distribution.

Marvin McKenzie

Scientology

Seventh-Day Adventist

Shinto

Two by Two's (Christian Conventions)

Unification Church (Moonies)

Unitarian Universalist Association

United Church of Christ/Congregational/Puritan/
Pilgrim

United Pentecostal Church International (UPCI)

Unity School of Christianity

The Way International

Worldwide Church of God (1968),

DENOMINATIONS-Lesson 1

What Do Independent Baptists Believe?

J**ude 3-4**

Origin: Baptistic Churches have existed since the time of Jesus Christ. Baptists are not protestants, having pre-dated the reformation by at least 1200 years. In 253 A.D. the bishop of the Church in Rome called the bishops from the Churches in Asia Minor "Anabaptists" because they would not accept members into their Churches who had "heretical baptism". For more information read <u>The Trail Of Blood</u> by J.M. Carroll, available from Ashland Avenue Baptist Church, Lexington, KY.

Doctrinal Beliefs:

1. The Bible

A. Every word of the original Scriptures was inspired by God. <u>II Timothy 3:16</u>

B. God preserved His Word for the English speaking people of the world in the King James Version of 1611. <u>Psalms 12:6-7</u>, <u>Matthew 5:18</u>

2. Salvation

A. By faith only, no works accepted or needed. <u>Ephesians 2:8-9</u>, <u>Titus 3:5</u>

B. Only through the atoning blood of Jesus. <u>I Peter 1:18-19</u>

C. By believing in your heart Jesus died for you and calling upon Him as Lord to save you. <u>Romans 10:9-10, 13</u>

D. Salvation for whosoever will. <u>John 3:16</u>, <u>Romans 10:13</u>

3. Baptism

A. For believers only, is not part of salvation. <u>Acts 8:12, 35-39</u>

Infant baptism is not found or practiced anywhere in the Bible.

B. By immersion only. <u>Acts 8:38-39</u>, <u>Matthew 3:16-17</u>

C. Brings a person into local Church membership. <u>Acts 2:41</u>

4. The Church

A. The only Scriptural Church is a local body of Christ, made up of baptized believers.

<u>I Corinthians 1:1-2,12:27</u>, <u>Colossians 1:18</u>

There is no universal, invisible Church. <u>Galatians 1:2</u>, <u>Revelation 1:11</u>

B. Baptism and the Lord's Supper are ordinances given to the local Church. <u>Acts 2:41, 20:7</u> They are commemorative only, having no part in salvation. <u>I Corinthians 1:17-18, 11:23-25</u>

C. The local Church has two scriptural officers: Pastor (Bishop, Elder, Overseer) <u>Ephesians 4:1-12</u>, <u>I Timothy 3:1</u>, <u>I Peter 5:1-3</u>, <u>Acts 20:17, 28</u>, and Deacon. <u>Philippians 1:1</u>

5. Jesus Christ

A. He was/is Eternal Creator God. <u>John 17:5, 1:1-3 & 10</u>, <u>Hebrews 1:1-2</u>

B. He was born of a virgin as God in the flesh. <u>Matthew 1:22-25</u>, <u>John 1:14</u>, <u>Colossians 1:19, 2:9</u>

C. He lived a perfect life fulfilling the law for us. <u>I Peter 2:21-23</u>, <u>Matthew 5:17</u>

D. His substitutionary death on the cross paid for the sins of all mankind. <u>I John 2:1-2</u>, <u>Hebrews 9:26</u>

E. He will return for His saints before the tribulation period. <u>I Thessalonians 4:16-18, 5:9-10</u>

6. The Trinity (Godhead)

A. Father, Son & Holy Spirit are all one. <u>I John 5:7</u>, <u>II Corinthians 13:14</u>

B. All three are Eternal God. <u>Genesis 1:1-2, 26-27</u>, <u>Hebrews 9:14, 13:8</u>

7. Heaven And Hell

A. Hell is a literal place where those who have not believed in and received Jesus Christ as their Savior go when they die to be tormented in literal fire forever. John 3:16-18, Luke 16:22-24, Matthew 23:33, 37

B. Heaven is a literal place where those who have received Jesus will have a home and rewards for serving God after they were saved. John 14:1-3

DENOMINATIONS-Lesson 2

Traits Of False Denominations

———

Matthew 7:15-23

1. Two causes of False Denominations

A. Satan starts False Denominations to deceive <u>Revelation 2:9</u>, <u>2 John 7, 9-11</u>

B. Once True Denominations have departed from the faith <u>1 Timothy 4:1-3</u>, <u>2 Corinthians 11:1-4</u>, <u>2 Peter 2:1-3</u>

2. Scripturally, what makes a Denomination False?

A. A False Doctrine of Jesus Christ <u>II John 7-11</u>, <u>II Peter 2:1-2</u>, <u>I John 2:22</u>

(1) Those who hold this doctrine are called "deceivers and an antichrist" (II John 7), "false teachers" (II Peter 2:1) and "Liar...antichrist, that denieth the Father" (I John 2:22).

(2) They attack the deity, virgin birth, sinless life, miracles, atoning death, physical resurrection, intercession and second coming of Jesus Christ. <u>John 8:41, 10:33</u>, <u>Matthew 9:34</u>, <u>Luke 23:35</u>, <u>Matthew 27:63</u>, <u>II Peter 3:3-4</u> Also see <u>Colossians 2:6-9</u>.

B. A False Gospel of Works Salvation <u>Galatians 1:6-9, 3:1-3</u>

(1) Those who "preach any other gospel" do "pervert the gospel of Christ" and are called "accursed". (Galatians 1:6-9)

(2) This "other gospel" told them that they were saved and "perfected" by keeping the law. (Galatians 3:1-3) See also <u>Galatians 2:16, 3:26</u> and <u>Matthew 7:21-23</u>.

C. Either of these false doctrines will classify a group as a False Denomination Scripturally, but many times they are found together. Groups that hold these doctrines are deceiving millions who trust in them for salvation. <u>Matthew 23:13, 15</u>

3. Other traits shared by many False Denominations:

A. Extra-Biblical Scripture <u>Revelation 22:18-19</u>, <u>Deuteronomy 4:2</u>

Their own Bible translation or other writings considered inspired: New World Translation, Book of Mormon, Koran, Science and Health, etc.

B. Prophet(s) or Teacher(s) Above or Equal to Jesus Christ

<u>Matthew 24:4-5, 11</u>, <u>I John 4:1</u> Joseph Smith, Brigham Young, Mary Baker Eddy, Buddha, Mohammed, Sun Yung Moon, the Pope, Baha'u'llah, etc.

C. Exclusiveness-Their group is the only correct way; all others are wrong. No church or group is the way; Jesus is the only way! <u>John 14:6</u>, <u>Acts 4:12</u>, <u>Romans 5:1</u>

D. Closed Meetings and Secret Ceremonies; non-members or only certain members may attend. <u>John 18:20-21</u>

DENOMINATIONS-Lesson 3

Baha'i Faith

A

Origin: "The Bahá'í Faith began with the mission entrusted by God to two Divine Messengers—the Báb and Bahá'u'lláh...The line of succession, referred to as the Covenant, went from Bahá'u'lláh to His Son 'Abdu'l-Bahá, and then from 'Abdu'l-Bahá to His grandson, Shoghi Effendi, and the Universal House of Justice, ordained by Bahá'u'lláh. A Bahá'í accepts the divine authority of the Báb and Bahá'u'lláh and of these appointed successors." (1) Today the Baha'is number over 8 million in 230 countries, with 177,000 in 7,000 communities in the United States. World headquarters are in Haifa, Israel.

Doctrinal Beliefs:

1. The Bible

A. The Christian Bible is superseded by the writings of their prophets; "You must realize that many of the things in the New Testament were written long after Jesus died, hence it is impossible to have absolute accuracy in everything. It would be natural for His followers to assert such things, but the revelation of Baha'u'llah supersedes such claims." (2) (Pg 255)

B. "The writings of the Báb and Bahá'u'lláh are regarded as Divine Revelation. The writings of Abdu'l-Bahá are recognised as sacred. The scriptures of other faiths, which include the teachings of previous Manifestations of God (Buddha, Moses, Jesus, Muhammad) are also regarded as Divine Revelations." (3)

C. Proof texts: Mark 13:31, Proverbs 30:5-6

2. Salvation

A. "...by the practice of principles laid down by Baha'u'llah and by making every effort through prayer and personal sacrifice to live in accord with the character of the divine being revealed in him, we arrive at <u>eventual salvation</u>...” (2) (pg 256) = Salvation by works!

B. When a Bahai teacher was asked if he knew his sins were forgiven and he had a place in the kingdom of God, he said, “I don't believe <u>any person</u> can make that statement...<u>I could not at the moment say this for myself</u>, but I <u>hope</u> that this will be the case when I die.” (2)(pg 256)=They cannot <u>know</u> that they are saved!

C. “An individual becomes a Bahá'í when he or she believes that Bahá'u'lláh is the Messenger of God for this age.” (4)

D. Proof texts: <u>Ephesians 2:8-9</u>, <u>I John 5:11-13</u>

3. Baptism “We have no 'baptismal service' in the Cause, such as the Christians have.” (5) <u>Matthew 28:18-20</u>

4. The Church

A. “Each year, the Baha'i community elects local and national councils, known as Spiritual Assemblies...In place of clergy or priesthood, these local assemblies ensure community members feel cared for and connected to one another. An international council, known as the Universal House of Justice[1], is elected once every five years.” (6)(Organization)

B. Proof texts: <u>Matthew 16:18</u>, <u>Ephesians 4:11-12</u>

5. Jesus Christ

A. “...we believe that Jesus was <u>only one of nine</u> manifestations of divine being” (2)(pg 254) “...Moses, Buddha, Zoroaster, Confucius, Christ, Mohammed, Krishna, Lowe and Baha'u'llah <u>are all equal</u> manifestations of the divine mind.” (2)(pg 255) Jesus equal with 8 other prophets!

B. “Christians may find spiritual peace in <u>believing in substitutionary atonement</u>. In Bahaism this is <u>unnecessary</u>.” (2)(pg 255)

---

1. http://universalhouseofjustice.bahai.org/

C. "The <u>alleged Resurrection</u> and <u>His Ascension</u> into heaven <u>may or may not be true</u> depending on your point of view." (2)(pg 255)

D. Proof texts: <u>John 14:6</u>, <u>I Corinthians 15:1-4</u>, <u>I John 2:1-2</u>

6. The Trinity (Godhead)

A. "If by the Trinity you mean the Christian concept that the <u>three persons, Father, Son and Holy Spirit, are all the one God</u>, the answer is <u>No</u>. We believe that God is one person in agreement with Judaism and Islam." (2)(pg 254)

B. "I believe that it is in your Gospel of John that Jesus promised another <u>Comforter</u> who would abide always. We understand this to be the <u>coming of Baha'u'llah</u>, a direct fulfillment of the words of Jesus." (2)(pg 256)

D. Proof Texts: <u>II Corinthians 13:14</u>, <u>John 14:16-17</u>

7. Heaven And Hell

A. "We do believe in the paradise of God which will be the abode of the <u>righteous</u> and in the resurrection and the final writing of all things." (2)(pg 256)

B. "We know <u>nothing</u> of eternal flames where sinners will be confined forever without respite." (2)(pg 256)

C. Proof texts: <u>Matthew 25:41</u>, <u>Isaiah 66:23-24</u>

THE BAHA'I FAITH ARE DEFINITELY A FALSE DENOMINATION, HAVING A FALSE DOCTRINE OF JESUS CHRIST AND A FALSE DOCTRINE OF SALVATION. THEY MUST BELIEVE IN BAHA'U'LLAH AND WORK FOR THEIR SALVATION.

---

(1) https://www.bahai.org/beliefs/bahaullah-covenant

(2) <u>The Kingdom of the Cults</u>, Walter Martin, published by Bethany Fellowship Inc., Minneapolis, Minnesota, 1965, 1977, 1985, 1997.

(3) https://www.bbc.co.uk/religion/religions/bahai/texts/texts.shtml

(4) https://www.upliftingwords.org/post/how-to-become-a-bahai

(5) https://bahaiquotes.com/subject/baptism

(6) http://www.bahai.us/beliefs

DENOMINATIONS-Lesson 4

Brethren (Church of the Brethren)

I **I Timothy 4:1-4**

Origin: "In 1708, Alexander Mack and seven others...baptized themselves in the Eder River near Schwarzenau, Germany, because they were influenced by the Anabaptists who strongly rejected infant baptism in favor of believer's baptism, and the Pietists." (1) Pietists came from "Lutheran and Reformed churches in Germany and the Anglican Church in England...Pietism stresses conversion and a personal experience of salvation, Bible study, devotional life, evangelical witness and a continuous openness to new light." (2) The groups that have resulted from that beginning in 1708 are: Church of the Brethren, Brethren Church, Grace Brethren, Dunkard Brethren and the Old German Baptist Brethren. Their beliefs, practices and theology are similar.

Doctrinal Beliefs: Brethren have stated that they have "no creed but Christ", and "the New Testament is our rule of faith and practice". (2)

1.The Bible

A. "Accepts and teaches the inspiration of the Bible (II Timothy 3:16)" (3)

B. "Maintains the New Testament as its only creed" (3)

C. John David Bowman wrote "the Brethren are more apt to appeal to 'the mind of Christ' than to the Bible. What is most important about the Bible is not whether it may contain errors, but that it does contain truth." (2)

D. "We are not yet agreed on whether inspiration is a finished or continuing process." Church of the Brethren-Statement, 1979 Annual Conference

E. Proof texts: Psalms 12:6-7, Revelation 22:18-19

2. Salvation

A. "Baptism of penitent believers by triune immersion <u>for the remission of sins</u>." (3) In explaining their logo, which contains waves of water, they state, "Water represents baptism through which a candidate enters into new life...we bury our sins and rise to newness of life in baptism." (4)

B. They believe that the Holy Spirit indwells you <u>after</u> your baptism: "Immediately following the baptism, while the candidate is still kneeling in the water, the minister lays hands upon the head of the new member and prays for the infilling of the Holy Spirit." (2)

C. Proof Texts: <u>Acts 16:30-31</u>, <u>Romans 10:9-15</u> (no baptism), <u>Romans 8:9</u>

3.Baptism

A. "Following the administration of the baptismal vows, the candidate kneels in front of the minister, and is then 'dunked' or immersed three times forward in the name of the Father, the Son, and the Holy Spirit. This...is what earned the Brethren the nickname 'Dunkers'." (2)

B. "Because Brethren hold to an ideal of 'no force in religion', they do not baptize infants." (2)

C. See "2. A" above, they believe that baptism is part of your salvation.

D. Proof texts: <u>Acts 2:41</u>, <u>Luke 23:39-43</u>

4. The Church

A. Brethren believe that "the Church is the body of Christ present in the world today with a mission of witness, service, and reconciliation." (3)

B. "...the Church of the Brethren is part of the worldwide body of Christ...We affirm the ways the Church of the Brethren has engaged and continues to be represented in ecumenical bodies..." (6)

C. Proof texts: <u>Matthew 28:18-20</u>, <u>I Timothy 3:15</u>, <u>II Corinthians 6:14</u>

5. Jesus Christ

A. They believe in the "virgin birth of Christ, the deity of Christ, the sin-pardoning value of His atonement, His resurrection, ascension, and personal and visible return". (3)

B. Proof texts: <u>Matthew 1:18</u>, <u>Colossians 2:8-9</u>, <u>Ephesians 1:7</u>, <u>Acts 1:9-11</u>

6. The Trinity (Godhead)

A. "As do most other Christians, the Brethren believe in God as Creator and loving Sustainer. We confess the Lordship of Christ, and we seek to be guided by the Holy Spirit in every aspect of life, thought, and mission." (7)

B. See "3.A" above. They baptize "three times forward in the name of the Father, the Son, and the Holy Spirit.

C. Proof Texts: <u>1 John 5:7</u>

7. Heaven And Hell

A. They believe that "the penalty for sin is separation in hell" and "Jesus promised the righteous a place in heaven". (5)

B. Proof Texts: <u>Revelation 20:12, 15</u>, <u>John 14:2-3</u>

THIS GROUP HAS A CORRECT DOCTRINE OF JESUS CHRIST, BUT BELIEVES THAT BAPTISM IS WHAT SAVES. A WORKS BASED SALVATION MAKES THEM A FALSE RELIGION. THEY DISAGREE WITH US ON 4 OF 7 DOCTRINES.

---

(1) <u>Who are the Brethren?</u> http://cob-net.org/membership.htm#whobrethren

(2) <u>Frequently Asked Questions About the Church of the Brethren</u>, https://cob-net.org/faqs.htm

(3) <u>The Brethren Card</u>, sanctioned in 1932 with the provision "that it must not be considered a creed". http://cob-net.org/bcard.htm

(4) <u>Church of the Brethren Logo</u> http://cob-net.org/logo.htm

(5) <u>Plan Of Redemption</u>, http://cob-net.org/plan.htm

(6) <u>2018 Vision Of Ecumenism For The 21st Century</u> https://www.brethren.org/ac/statements/2018-vision-of-ecumenism-for-the-21st- century/

(7) <u>What We Believe</u>, https://www.brethren.org/about/beliefs/

DENOMINATIONS-Lesson 5

Buddhist

Isaiah 8:20

Origin: Siddhartha Gautama is born in 560 B.C., a Hindu prince in Nepal near the border of India. When 29 years old he left his wife and child to find "the true meaning of human life". After 6 years of struggles and searching he found the "path to enlightenment" and became Buddha (the Perfectly Enlightened One). There are over 300 million Buddhists today divided into three main sects. The Thervada (Hinayana-doctrine of the lesser way) believe that Nirvana is only possible for the closest followers of Buddha. The Mahayana (doctrine of the greater way) believe Nirvana is possible for all people through Buddha and other savior gods. This form entered Japan in the 6th century B.C. and became Zen Buddhism. The Vajrayana (Tibet) believe in spells, incantations and magical words to protect from demons (demon worship). Their leader is the Dalai Lama.

Doctrinal Beliefs:

1. The Bible

A. "The truest of books can be at best a finger pointing at the moon. If we fix our gaze on the finger, we miss the heavenly glory." (1)(pg 236)

B. Major Scriptures are: The Tripitaka, Anguttara-Nikaya, Dhammapada, Sutta-Nipata, Samutta-Nikaya and many others.

C. Proof texts: Psalms 119:105,130,140

2. Salvation

A. Buddhism teaches "Four Noble Truths: 1. The Truth Of Suffering...2. The Cause Of Suffering...3. The freedom From Suffering...4. The Path Of Liberation From Suffering" (2)

B. "The Eightfold Path of liberation from suffering...1. right view, 2. right intention, 3. right action, 4. right speech, 5. right livelihood, 6. right effort, 7. right mindfulness and 8. right meditation." (2) "Buddha claimed that whoever could follow this Eightfold Path would eventually reach Nirvana, a release from the endless cycle of death and rebirth." (3)(pg 107-108)

C. "Buddha...denied that man has an atman (soul)." (3)(pg 106)

D. Proof texts: Titus 3:5, Galatians 2:16

3. Baptism Not practiced to my knowledge. Matthew 28:18-20

4. The Church

A. "The Sangha literally means community, assembly or association in Sanskrit. It is a group of people normally Buddhist monks and nuns who teach and uphold the teachings of Buddha to others. They are people who have at least attained one of the four levels of Enlightenment." (2) (Sangha)

B. Proof text: Philippians 1:1

5. Jesus Christ

A. Buddhists say about Jesus Christ that he was "a good teacher, less important than Buddha." (3)(pg 116)

B. Buddhism "rejects the necessity of personal redemption from the penalty of sin revealed in the Person of Jesus Christ". (1)(pg 238)

C. Jesus did not bodily rise from the dead, they believe in reincarnation.

D. "Just as all men and women of all the people of the earth have said and will say at the moment of their Awakening, so do we say simply, 'I am the way'". (1)(pg 237)

E. Proof texts: John 14:6, 3:36

6. The Trinity (Godhead)

A. "Buddhists deny the existence of a personal God". (3)(pg 116) "Buddha is agnostic". (3)(pg 113) An agnostic doubts the existence of God.

B. Buddhism "supersedes the doctrine of a real Creator". (1)(pg 239)

C. "The Holy Spirit...this is 'Satori', which is enlightenment. Example of this phenomenon: After his master Matsu abruptly took hold of his nose, he gave it a twist. This made his back wet with cold perspiration. He was said to have Satori." (1)(pg 237)

D. Proof Texts: <u>Genesis 1:1-2</u>, <u>Matthew 3:16-17</u>

7. Heaven And Hell

A. Buddhists believe in "Nirvana, a release from the endless cycle of death and rebirth." (3)(pg107-108)

B. Do not believe in a literal heaven or hell. "Immaculate Yogins do not enter Nirvana and the precept-violating monks do not go to hell." (1)(pg 237) "...the mind is its own place, and of itself can make a heaven of hell, and a hell of heaven." (1)(pg 240)

C. Proof texts: <u>I Thessalonians 4:16-17</u>, <u>Revelation 20:10</u>

THE BUDDHISTS ARE DEFINITELY A FALSE RELIGION, NOT HAVING A CORRECT DOCTRINE OF JESUS CHRIST OR A CORRECT DOCTRINE OF SALVATION. THEY TEACH THE FOUR NOBLE TRUTHS AND FOLLOW THE NOBLE EIGHTFOLD PATH TO ATTAIN NIRVANA (SALVATION).

---

(1) <u>The Kingdom of the Cults</u>, Walter Martin, published by Bethany Fellowship Inc., Minneapolis, Minnesota, 1965, 1977, 1985, 1997.

(2) <u>Teachings Of The Buddha</u>, https://teachingsofthebuddha.com/the-four-noble-truths- and-the-eightfold-path-explained/

(3) <u>So What's The Difference?</u>, Fritz Ridenour, published by Regal Books Division, G/L Publications, Glendale, California, 1967.

DENOMINATIONS-Lesson 6

Christian and Missionary Alliance

I **John 4:1**

Origin: "The Christian and Missionary Alliance developed from the work of Albert B. Simpson (died 1919), a Presbyterian minister who left Presbyterianism to become an independent evangelist in New York City...In 1887 Simpson and others organized two societies, one for domestic activities and one for foreign missions, which were merged to form the Christian and Missionary Alliance in 1897... In 2004 the group reported more than 500,000 members and nearly 2,000 congregations in North America." (1)

Doctrinal Beliefs:

1. The Bible

A. "The Old and New Testaments, <u>inerrant as originally given</u>, were verbally inspired by God and are a complete revelation of His will for the salvation of men...constitute the divine and only rule of Christian faith and practice." (2)

B. They use many different translations (NASB, NIV, NIRV, NKJV, CJB) in the verses quoted in their explanation of the "Fourfold Gospel" (3)

C. In the NIV "hell" is left out 39 times and references to Jesus as "Lord" are removed 24 times.

D. In the NASB "hell" is deleted 39 times and the NIRV leaves out the "blood" of Jesus" 5 times.

E. Proof texts: <u>Revelation 22:19, Colossians 1:2 & 14</u>

2. Salvation

A. "Salvation has been provided through Jesus Christ for all men; and those who repent and believe in Him are born again of the Holy Spirit, receive the gift of eternal life, and they become children of God." (2)

B. "All men are born with a sinful nature...and can be saved only through the atoning work of the Lord Jesus Christ." (2)

C. "It is the will of God that each believer should be filled with the Holy Spirit and be <u>sanctified wholly</u>...This is both a crisis and progressive experience wrought in the life of the believer <u>subsequent to conversion</u>." (2) (Whole sanctification after conversion, is not Scriptural.)

D. "Though some may speak in tongues when they are filled with the Holy Spirit, others do not." (4)

E. Proof text: <u>I Corinthians 2:12</u>, <u>II Corinthians 5:17</u>

3. Baptism

A. "Baptism followed repentance and faith in New Testament times." (3)

B. "Because of the meaning of the word baptize and the mode of the first baptisms...Alliance churches practice baptism by immersion." (5)

C. "In cases where immersion is impossible due to physical limitations, an alternate mode is acceptable." (5)

D. Proof Text: <u>Acts 8:12</u>

4. The Church

A. "The Church consists of <u>all those who believe</u> in the Lord Jesus Christ" (2)(Universal, invisible Church)

B. "The local church is a body of believers in Christ who are joined together for the worship of God, for edification through the Word of God, for prayer, fellowship, the proclamation of the gospel, and observance of the ordinances of Baptism and the Lord's Supper." (2)

C. Proof Texts: <u>Galatians 1:1-2</u>

5. Jesus Christ

A. "Jesus Christ is true God and true man. He was conceived by the Holy Spirit and born of the Virgin Mary. He died upon the cross, the Just for the un-just, as a substitutionary sacrifice, and all who believe in Him are justified on the ground of His shed blood. He arose from the dead according to the Scriptures. He is now at the right hand of the Majesty on high as our great High Priest. He will come again to establish His kingdom of righteousness and peace." (2)

B. Proof Text: Matthew 1:19-21

6. The Trinity (Godhead)

A. "There is one God, who is infinitely perfect, existing eternally in three persons: Father, Son and Holy Spirit." (2)

B. Proof Text: Titus 3:4-6

7. Heaven And Hell

A. "The portion of the impenitent and unbelieving person is existence forever in conscious torment; and that of the believer, in everlasting joy and bliss." (2)

B. "There shall be a bodily resurrection of the just and of the unjust; for the former, a resurrection unto life; for the latter, a resurrection unto judgment."(2)

C. Proof Text: John 5:28-29

THIS GROUP IS NOT A WHOLLY FALSE DENOMINATION. BUT THEY USE THE CORRUPT MODERN ENGLISH TRANSLATIONS AND DIVERGE FROM CORRECT BIBLICAL DOCTRINE IN THE MATTERS OF ENTIRE SANCTIFICATION AFTER SALVATION, ALLOWED MODES OF BAPTISM AND THE UNIVERSAL CHURCH.

---

(1)Christian And Missionary Alliance, https://www.britannica.com/topic/Christian-and-Missionary-Alliance

(2) The Alliance Statement Of Faith, (2022 Revision) https://cmalliance.org/who-we-are/what-we-believe/statement-of-faith/

(3) <u>The Fourfold Gospel</u>, https://awf.world/the-fourfold-gospel/

(4) <u>What is the evidence of being filled with the Holy Spirit?</u>, https://cmalliance.org/who-we-are/what-we-believe/perspectives/

(5) <u>Baptism</u> https://www.myfac.org/baptism-2/

DENOMINATIONS-Lesson 7

Christian Church (Disciples of Christ) / Church of Christ

———

I **Corinthians 1:17-18**

Origin: "In 1804, in the western frontier state of Kentucky, Barton W. Stone and several other Presbyterian preachers took...action declaring that they would take the Bible as the 'only sure guide to heaven'. Thomas Campbell, and his illustrious son, Alexander Campbell, took similar steps in the year 1809 in what is now the state of West Virginia...Although these movements were completely independent in their beginnings eventually they became one strong restoration movement because of their common purpose and plea. These men did not advocate the starting of a new church, but rather a return to Christ's church as described in the Bible...The most recent dependable estimate lists more than 15,000 individual churches of Christ. The "Christian Herald," a general religious publication which presents statistics concerning all the churches, estimates that the total membership of the churches of Christ is now 2,000,000." (1) The Christian Church (DOC) had 3627 congregations and 350,618 members in 2020.

Doctrinal Beliefs:

1. The Bible

A. The Church of Christ "...Believes all the Bible to be the inspired Word of God" (2)(pg 51)

B. The Christian Church (DOC) "...lay stress on New Testament Authority, reject creeds and confessions of faith..." (3)(pg 757)

C. Versions found quoted in research are ASV, NASB, TEV, NKJV, and KJV.

D. Proof texts: Psalms 12:6-7

2. Salvation

A. "Alexander Campbell...laid much stress on the baptismal act as connected with the remission of sins." (3)(pg 701)

B. "Any church which is not essential to man's salvation is not Christ's church, because membership in his church is indispensable to salvation." (2)(pg 186)

C. "The Bible teaches that a child of God can fall and be lost." (2)(pg 143)

D. Proof Texts: Luke 23:39-43, John 5:24

3. Baptism

A. " Through baptism into Christ we enter into newness of life and are made one with the whole people of God." (4)

B. "VI. Why be baptized?...11. To wash away your sins." (2)(pg 138-139)

C. "It is in baptism, in this age, that man comes in contact with the saving blood." (2)(pg 114)

D. Proof Texts: Matthew 28:19-20, I Corinthians 1:17-18

4. The Church

A. " 2. Within the universal Body of Christ, the Christian Church (Disciples of Christ) is identifiable by its testimony, tradition, name..." (4)

B. "In each congregation...there is a plurality of elders or presbyters who serve as the governing body. These men are selected by the local congregations ...Serving under the elders are deacons, teachers, and evangelists..." (5)

C. "...they practise weekly communion as Apostolic." (3)(pg 757)

D. Proof texts: Philippians 1:1, 2 Corinthians 1:1

5. Jesus Christ

A. "As members of the Christian Church we confess that Jesus is the Christ, the Son of the living God, and proclaim him Lord and Savior of the world". (4)

B. "II. Christ's blood was shed for human redemption." (2)(pg 112)

C. "1...All dominion in the church belongs to Jesus, its Lord and head, and any exercise of authority in the church on earth stands under His judgment." (4)

D. Proof Text: <u>I John 1:1-3</u>

6. The Trinity (Godhead)

A. "Alexander Campbell...repudiated all formal statements of the doctrine of the Trinity...and insisted that the Holy Spirit operates only through the word." (3)(pg. 701) (Today, the doctrine of the Trinity of the Godhead is seldom mentioned and belief varies greatly in both groups.)

B. Proof Texts: <u>I John 5:7</u>, <u>II Corinthians 13:14</u>

7. Heaven And Hell

A. "The Kingdom has been established and Christ is now reigning." (2)(pg 86) "Therefore, the Kingdom came on Pentecost." (2)(pg 88) (No future 1000-year reign of Christ!)

B. "The statement of Christ in Matthew 25, and elsewhere, are taken at face value. It is believed that after death each man must come before God in judgment and that he will be judged according to the deeds done while he lived. After judgment is pronounced, he will spend eternity either in heaven or hell." (6)

C. Proof Texts: <u>Revelation 20:1-6</u>

THIS GROUP IS A FALSE DENOMINATION THAT BELIEVES A PERSON CAN ONLY BE SAVED BY BELIEVING IN JESUS CHRIST <u>AND</u> BEING BAPTIZED BY THEM. THEY ALSO DO NOT BELIEVE IN THE TRINITY OR ETERNAL SECURITY OF THE BELIEVER.

(1) <u>The Historical Background Of The Restoration Movement</u>, https://www.church-of-christ.org/who

(2) <u>Why I Am A Member Of The Church Of Christ</u>, Leroy Brownlow, Brownlow Publishing Company, Inc., Fort Worth, Texas, 1945, 1973

(3) <u>A Manual Of Church History</u>, Volume II, Albert Henry Newman, Judson Press, Valley Forge, 1902, 1931, 1972

(4) <u>The Design Of The Christian Church (Disciples Of Christ)</u>, preamble,

https://cdn.disciples.org/wp-content/uploads/2013/06/06162227/TheDesign-1.pdf

(5) <u>How Are The Churches Of Christ Governed</u>? https://www.church-of-christ.org/how-are-the-churches-of-christ-governed.html

(6) <u>Does The Church Of Christ Believe In Heaven And Hell</u>? https://www.church-of-christ.org/does-the-church-of-christ-believe-in-heaven-and-hell.html

DENOMINATIONS-Lesson 8

Christian Identity Movement

<u>Galatians 3:28</u>

Origin: "The term 'Christian Identity' expresses their belief, supposedly based in Christianity, that the 'identity' of the White race is that it is God's chosen people...We believe the White, Anglo-Saxon, Germanic and kindred people to be God's true, literal Children of Israel...This chosen seedline making up the 'Christian Nations'...of the earth stands far superior to all other peoples in their call as God's servant race" (1) "The largest Christian Identity movement has traditionally been the Ku Klux Klan, which was reorganized in 1915...Other current organizations which follow Christian Identity beliefs are: American Nazi Party; Aryan Nations; Church Of Jesus Christ-Aryan Nations; Posse Comitatus; Christian Posse Comiatus; Confederate Hammerskins; Jubilee-National Assoc. for the Advancement of White People; The Order...Scriptures for America; White Aryan Resistance (WAR); and White Separatist Banner" (2) "Membership: less than 50,000 in America only." (3)

Doctrinal Beliefs:

1. The Bible

A. "WE BELIEVE the entire Bible, both Old and New Testaments, as originally inspired, to be the inerrant, supreme, revealed Word of God. The history, covenants, and prophecy of this Holy Book were written for and about a specific elect family of people who are the children of YHVH God...through the seedline of Adam" (4)

B. "Texts: Old and New Testaments of the Bible, some think sections of the U.S. Constitution were divinely inspired." (3)

C. "Identity teachers of today such as Pastor Arnold Murray maintain the great Pyramid was built by the Israelites and is a second revelation of God." (5)

D. "a very conservative interpretation of the Christian Bible...this leads to...a view of the white race, the "Adamic race"... as superior." (2)

E. Proof texts: Proverbs 30:5-6

2.cSalvation

A. "WE BELIEVE salvation is by grace through faith, not of works. Eternal life is the gift of God through redemption that is in our Savior Yahshua (Jesus Christ)..." (4)

B. "WE BELIEVE Yahshua the Messiah (Jesus the Christ) came to redeem ...only His people Israel who are His portion and inheritance." (4)

C. "WE BELIEVE God chose unto Himself a special race of people that are above all people upon the face of the earth...The descendants of the twelve sons of Jacob, called 'Israel'...electing out of all twelve tribes those who inherit the Kingdom of God...WE BELIEVE the White, Anglo-Saxon, Germanic and kindred people to be God's true, literal Children of Israel." (4)

D. Christian Identity beliefs...Wesley Swift formulated the doctrine which states that non-Caucasian peoples have no souls and therefore they can never earn God's favor or be saved. (6)

E. Proof Texts: Romans 1:16, Romans 10:12-13

3. Baptism

A. "WE BELIEVE in water baptism by immersion according to the Scriptures for all true believers; being buried into the death of Yahshua the Messiah (Jesus Christ) for the remission of our sins...Baptism being ordained of God a testimony to the New Covenant as circumcision was under the Old Covenant." (4)

B. Proof Texts: Acts 8:12, Galatians 3:27-28

4. The Church

A. "WE BELIEVE Yahshua the Messiah (Jesus Christ) to be…head over His body of called-out saints, the Church…His bride, the wife of the Lamb, is the twelve tribes of the children of Israel." (4)

B. "Christian Identity is strongest in the Pacific Northwest and the Midwest, but Christian Identity groups or churches can be found in virtually every region of the United States…" (7)

D. Proof texts: <u>Colossians 1:1-2, 3:11</u>

5. Jesus Christ

A. "WE BELIEVE that God the Son, Yahshua the Messiah (Jesus Christ), became man in order to redeem His people Israel…died as the Passover Lamb of God on the Cross of Calvary finishing His perfect atoning sacrifice for the remission of our sins; He arose from the grave on the third day triumphing over death; and ascended into heaven where He is now reigning at the right hand of God." (4)

B. "…Jesus was not a Jew of the tribe of Judah, but an Aryan of the ten lost tribes of Israel and an ancestor of the present British, Germanic and Scandinavian people." (5)

C. Proof Text: <u>Luke 1:26-27, 32-33</u>, <u>Acts 17:24-26</u>

6. The Trinity (Godhead)

A. "WE BELIEVE in YHVH the one and only true and living eternal God; the God of our fathers Abraham, Isaac and Jacob, the Creator of all things who is omnipotent, omnipresent, unchangeable and all-knowing; the Great I AM who is manifested in three beings: God the Father, God the Son, and God the Holy Spirit, all one God." (4)

B. Proof Texts: <u>I John 5:7</u>, <u>II Corinthians 13:14</u>

7. Heaven And Hell

A. "Christian Identity…believes in the inevitability of the end of the world and the Second Coming of Christ. It is believed that these events are part of a cleansing process that is needed before Christ's kingdom can be established on earth. During this time, Jews and their allies will attempt to destroy the white race using any means available...Some contend there will be a race war in which millions will die; others believe that the United Nations, backed by Jewish representatives of the anti-Christ, will take over the country and promote a New World Order." (2)

B. "WE BELIEVE the ultimate destiny of all history will be the establishment of the Kingdom of God upon this earth with Yahshua our Messiah (Jesus Christ) reigning as King of kings over the house of Jacob forever...His elect Saints will be raised immortal at His return to rule and reign with Him as kings and priests." (4)

C. "Christian Identity promotes the idea that all non-whites (people who are not of wholly European descent) will either be exterminated or enslaved in order to serve the white race in the new Heavenly Kingdom on Earth under the reign of Jesus Christ. Its doctrine states that only "Adamic" (white) people can achieve salvation and enter paradise." (6)

D. "WE BELIEVE the United States of America fulfills the prophecied place where Christians from all the tribes of Israel would be regathered." (4)

E. Proof Texts: <u>Zechariah 12:2-3, 9</u>, <u>14:4, 16</u>, <u>Romans 11:25-28</u>

THESE GROUPS CLAIM TO BE CHRISTIAN, BUT TWIST EVERYTHING TO FIT THEIR RACIST AGENDA. THEY ARE A FALSE DENOMINATION ON THE BASIS THAT THEY SAY JESUS WAS NOT A JEW OF THE TRIBE OF JUDAH, BUT AN ARYAN AND THAT THEY LIMIT SALVATION TO THE WHITE RACE ONLY.

---

(1) <u>Christian Identity</u>, http://www.watchman.org/profiles/pdf/christianidentityprofile.pdf

(2) <u>Christian Identity Movement</u>, http://www.religioustolerance.org/cr_ident.htm

(3) <u>The Christian Identity Movement</u>, Christian Apologetics & Research Ministry

https://carm.org/christian-identity-movement

(4) <u>Doctrinal Statement of Beliefs</u>, Kingdom Identity Ministries-

http://www.kingidentity.com/doctrine.htm

(5) <u>Identity: A 'Christian' Religion for White Racists</u>, https://www.equip.org/articles/christian-identity-a-christian-religion-for-white-racists/

(6) <u>Christian Identity</u>, https://en.wikipedia.org/wiki/Christian_Identity

(7) <u>Christian Identity</u>, https://www.adl.org/resources/backgrounders/christian-identity?gclid=CjwKCAjw-rOaBhA9EiwAUkLV4i_OrAxMqZMQq2Cluf_2RMPbqg_VwqjEx 87ZwEu-ehHVMwGkhgiMqhoC5x8QAvD_BwE

DENOMINATIONS-Lesson 9

Church of Jesus Christ of Latter-day Saints (Mormons)

Matthew 15:9

Origin: This denomination was organized in 1830 in New York state by a 25-year-old man named Joseph Smith. He claimed to have been told by Moroni, a resurrected, glorified Nephite, of some gold tablets that recorded the history of his people in the Americas and how Jesus had visited them after His resurrection. Joseph Smith also states that Moroni taught him how to translate these gold plates, which became the Book of Mormon. The group moved to Kirtland, Ohio in 1833 and to Nauvoo, Illinois in 1839. Joseph Smith was killed in 1844. In 1846 Brigham Young led part of the group to what became Salt Lake City. 2021 membership was over 16 million. The rest of the group, under the leadership of Joseph Smith III, became the Reorganized Church of Jesus Christ of the Latter-day Saints in Independence, Missouri.

Doctrinal Beliefs:

1. The Bible

A. "8. We believe the Bible to be the word of God as far as it is translated correctly, we also believe the Book of Mormon to be the word of God." (1)

B. *The Doctrine and Covenants* claims on its title page: "Containing Revelations given through Joseph Smith the Prophet. With some Additions by his successors in the Presidency of the Church." (2)

C. "*The Pearl of Great Price*, A selection from the revelations, translations and narrations of Joseph Smith, First Prophet, Seer and Revelator." (Taken from the title page.) It contains "The Book of Moses", "The Book of Abraham", "Writings of Joseph Smith", and "The Articles of Faith". (3)

D. "Besides 'translating' the *Book of Mormon*, Joseph Smith 'revised' sections of the King James Bible. New revelations were added, especially in Genesis.

These additions, quoted in *The Pearl of Great Price*, state, for instance, that Satan wanted to redeem mankind but was refused by God, and that Adam was baptized by immersion. Also added to Genesis 50 was a prophecy about the coming of Joseph Smith, Jr. himself: 'And that seer I bless... and his name shall be called Joseph...for the thing which the Lord shall bring forth by his hand shall bring my people unto Salvation.' (Genesis 50:33, Inspired Version By Joseph Smith) Such scriptures are completely sacred to Mormons." (4)(pg159)

E. "9. We believe all that God has revealed, and that He does now reveal, and we believe that He will yet reveal many great and important things pertaining to the Kingdom of God." (1) (Continuing revelation)

F. Proof texts: <u>Deuteronomy 12:32</u>, <u>Proverbs 30:6</u>

2. Salvation

A. "3. We believe that through the atonement of Christ, all mankind may be saved, by obedience to the laws and ordinances of the Gospel." (1)

B. "4. We believe that the first principles and ordinances of the Gospel are: first, Faith in the Lord Jesus Christ; second, Repentance; third, Baptism by (18) immersion for the remission of sins; fourth, Laying on of hands for the gift of the Holy Ghost." (1) (They believe in salvation by faith plus works.)

C. Proof Texts: <u>Ephesians 2:8-9</u>, <u>Acts 16:30-31</u>

3. Baptism

A. *The Book of Mormon*, Moroni 8:10-11: "Behold I say unto you that this thing shall ye teach-repentance and baptism unto those who are accountable and capable of committing sin; yea, teach parents that they must repent and be baptized, and humble themselves as their little children, and they shall all be saved with their little children. And their little children need no repentance, neither baptism..." (5)

B. Concerning baptism for the dead, Joseph Smith writes in *Doctrine and Covenants*, Section 127:6-7; "Verily, thus saith the Lord unto you concerning your dead: When any of you are baptized for your dead, let there be a recorder, and let him be eyewitness of your baptisms...that in all your recordings it may be recorded in heaven." Also, section 128:5; "...by conforming to the ordinance...for the salvation of the dead who should die without a knowledge of the gospel". (2)

C. Proof Text: I Corinthians 1:14-18

4. The Church

A. "6. We believe in the same organization that existed in the Primitive Church, namely, apostles, prophets, pastors, teachers, evangelists, and so forth." (1)

B. *Doctrine and Covenants* states in section 107:1; "There are, in the church, two priesthoods, namely, the Melchizedek and Aaronic, including the Levitical Priesthood." Of the Melchizedek Priesthood in verse 5; "All other authorities or offices in the church are appendages to this priesthood." (2)

C. Proof text: Philippians 1:1

5. Jesus Christ

A. Brigham Young stated in *Journal of Discourses*, Vol. 1, pages 50-51; "When the Virgin Mary conceived the child Jesus, the Father had begotten him in his own likeness. He was not begotten by the Holy Ghost. And who was the Father?...Jesus, our elder brother was begotten in the flesh by the same character that was in the garden of Eden, and who is our Father in Heaven" (6)(Pg 186) (He is saying that God the Father was/is Adam.)

B. "In Mormon theology, Christ as a pre-existent spirit was not only the spirit brother of the devil (*The Pearl of Great Price*, Book of Moses, Chapter 4, verses 1-4; *Journal of Discourses*, Vol. 13:282), but celebrated his own marriage to 'both the Marys and Martha, whereby he could see his seed before he was crucified.' (Apostle Orson Hyde, *Journal of Discourses*, Vol. 4, pages 259-260)." (6)(Pg 192)

C. Proof text: John 1:1

6. The Trinity (Godhead)

A. "1. We believe in God, the Eternal Father, and in His Son, Jesus Christ, and in the Holy Ghost." (1)

B. "In his *Journal of Discourses*, Joseph Smith wrote, 'God himself was once as we are now and is an exalted man...'" (4)(pg 161)

C. Brigham Young stated, "When our father Adam came into the garden of Eden, he brought Eve, one of his wives with him...He is our FATHER and our GOD, and the only God with whom WE have to do." (6)(pg 186)

D. "The Father has a body of flesh and bones as tangible as man's; the Son also; but the Holy Ghost has not a body of flesh and bones, but is a personage of Spirit." (2)(Sec. 130:22)

E. "The truth of the matter is that Mormonism has never historically accepted the Christian doctrine of the Trinity..." (6)(Pg180)

F. Proof Texts: John 4:24, I John 5:7

7. Heaven And Hell

A. *Doctrine and Covenants* 131:1 says; "In the celestial glory there are three heavens or degrees" (2)

B. "Mormons also believe in the bodily resurrection of all men and in salvation in a three-fold heaven...the telestial, the terrestrial and the celestial. The first heaven is designed for heathen people who rejected the gospel and... suffering in hell, pending the last resurrection. The second heaven will be inhabited by Christians who did not accept the Mormon message, along with...other religions. The final or celestial heaven is itself divided into three kingdoms, the highest of which is godhood...having been sealed by celestial marriage in a Mormon temple...each who becomes a god will, with his family, rule a separate planet..." (6)(Pg 196) (Unbelievers are in Hell only until the last resurrection, and then all will believe.)

C. Proof Text: Luke 16:22-23, II Corinthians 12:2-4

THIS GROUP IS DEFINITELY A FALSE DENOMINATION, HAVING A DOCTRINE OF JESUS AS THE SON OF ADAM AND SALVATION BY REPENTANCE <u>AND</u> BAPTISM.

---

(1) <u>The Church of Jesus Christ of Latter-Day Saints</u>, <u>Articles of Faith</u>, Joseph Smith

http://www.bible.ca/cr-Mormons#lds

(2) <u>The Doctrine And Covenants Of The Church Of Jesus Christ Of Latter-Day Saints</u>,

Joseph Smith, Salt Lake City, Utah, 1974

(3) <u>The Pearl Of Great Price</u>, Joseph Smith, Salt Lake City, Utah, 1974

(4) <u>So What's The Difference?</u>, Fritz Ridenour, Published by Regal Books Division, G/L Publications, Glendale, California, 1970

(5) <u>The Book Of Mormon, Another Testament Of Jesus Christ</u>, The Church of Jesus Christ of Latter-day Saints, Salt Lake City, Utah, Copyright 1981 (First English printing, 1830)

(6) <u>The Kingdom of the Cults</u>, Walter Martin, published by Bethany Fellowship Inc., Minneapolis, Minnesota, 1965, 1977.

DENOMINATIONS-Lesson 10

Episcopal / Anglican (Church of England)

———

<u>M</u><u>ark 7:6-9</u>

Origin: "England adhered to the Catholic Church for almost a thousand years...but, in 1534, during the reign of King Henry VIII, the greater part of the church, through a series of legislative acts between 1533 and 1536 became independent from the Pope as the Church of England, with Henry declaring himself Supreme Head." (1) "The Church of England established itself in the English colonies...in Jamestown, Virginia, in 1607. The Episcopal Church was formally separated from the Church of England in 1789 so that clergy would not be required to accept the supremacy of the British monarch." (2) "The Episcopal Church...is a member church of the worldwide Anglican Communion" (2) "As of 2020, the Episcopal Church had 1,736,282 active baptized members..." (2) "in 2017, approximately 1.14 million people were a part of the regular worshipping community, meaning those attending church once a month or more" (2) (Church Of England)

1. The Bible

A. "The Holy Scriptures, commonly called the Bible, are the books of the Old and New Testaments; other books, called the Apocrypha, are often included in the Bible." (3)

B. "Holy Scripture containeth all things necessary to salvation: so that whatsoever is not read therein, nor may be proved thereby, is not to be required of any man, that it should be believed as an article of Faith." (4) (Article VI)

C. "The Episcopal Church has largely been taken over by modernism. A majority of the leaders hold rationalistic beliefs, denying the perfect inspiration of the Bible..." (5) (Pg 19)

D. "This Church uses two creeds: The Apostles' and the Nicene Creeds." (3)

E. Proof texts: <u>II Timothy 3:16-17</u>, <u>Deuteronomy 4:2</u>

2. Salvation

A. "We are accounted righteous before God, only for the merit of our Lord and Saviour Jesus Christ by Faith, and not for our own works…" (4) (Article XI)

B. "Baptism is union with Christ…birth into God's family the Church, forgiveness of sins, and new life in the Holy Spirit." (3) (Baptismal regeneration)

C. "Holy Communion is the Body and Blood of Christ given to his people…The benefits we receive are the forgiveness of our sins, the strengthening of our union with Christ…eternal life" (3)

D. "Penance, is the rite in which those who repent of their sins may confess them to God in the presence of a priest and receive assurance of pardon and the grace of absolution." (3) (Auricular confession)

E. "In June 2006, the national convention of the Episcopal Church in America voted overwhelmingly against a resolution stating "an unchanging commitment to Jesus…the only name by which any person may be saved. More than seven tenths of the House of Deputies rejected the motion. (5) (pg 21)

F. Proof Texts: <u>I Corinthians 1:17-18</u>, <u>11:24-25</u>, <u>I Timothy 2:5</u>

3. Baptism

A. Baptism is taught as being essential to their salvation. (see 2B)

B. "Infants are baptized so that they can share citizenship in the Covenant, membership in Christ, and redemption by God." (3) "The Baptism of young Children is…retained in the Church, as most agreeable with the institution of Christ." (4) (Article XXVII) (Infant baptism was NOT instituted by Christ!)

C. The Nicene Creed states, "We acknowledge one baptism for the forgiveness of sins " (6)

D. Proof texts: <u>Acts 16:30-34</u>, <u>18:8</u>

4. The Church

A. "The Church is the community of the New Covenant...The Church is described as one, holy, catholic, and apostolic." (3)

B. "Episcopal Church Government: Anglican church government is the unbiblical episcopal system—the local church is governed by outside control through a hierarchy of priests and bishops." (5) (Pg 2)

C. "The Episcopal Church...approved women's ordination to the priesthood in 1976. Today there are 1,070 ordained women in the denomination. The Episcopalians ordained the first Anglican female bishop in 1989." (5) (Pg 4)

D. "Episcopal Bishop John Spong said...'I regard the blessing of gay or lesbian couples by the church to be inevitable, right, and a positive good.' This immoral thinking apparently permeates the Episcopal denomination. In a 1993 study, 70% of nearly 20,000 Episcopalians surveyed said it is possible for sexually active homosexuals to be faithful Christians, and 75% of those surveyed said a faithful Christian can live with someone of the opposite sex without being married (*Christian News*, Nov. 1, 1993)." (5) (Pg 22)

E. Proof texts: <u>Revelation 1:10-11</u>, <u>I Corinthian 14:34</u>, <u>Romans 1:26-28</u>

5. Jesus Christ

A. The Nicene Creed says, "We believe in one Lord, Jesus Christ, the only Son of God, eternally begotten of the Father...true God from true God, begotten, not made, of one being with the Father. Through him all things were made. For us and our salvation he came down from heaven: by the power of the Holy Spirit he became incarnate from the Virgin Mary, and was made man. For our sake he was crucified...he suffered death and was buried. On the third day he rose again; he ascended into heaven and is seated at the right hand of the Father. He will come again in glory to judge the living and the dead, and his kingdom will have no end." (6)

B. "Bishop James Pike called the virgin birth of Christ a 'primitive myth' and said that Joseph was probably Jesus' real father" (5) (Pg 6)

C. "A poll of nearly 2,000 of the Church's 10,000 clergy found that...a third... doubt/disbelieve in the physical resurrection and only half are convinced of the truth of the virgin birth." (7) (Church Of England)

D. "A majority of the leaders hold rationalistic beliefs...denying or questioning Christ's deity, virgin birth, and resurrection...yet they are allowed to remain in good standing." (5) (Pg 19) (Episcopal Church)

E. Proof Text: Matthew 1:20-25

6. The Trinity (Godhead)

A. "And in unity of this Godhead there are three persons, of one substance, power, and eternity; the Father, the Son and the Holy Ghost." (4) (Article I)

B. Episcopal Bishop James Pike said, "I have abandoned ship on the doctrine of the Trinity. (*Christian Beacon*, Mar. 17. 1955)" (5) (Pg 19)

C. Proof text: II Corinthians 13:14

7. Heaven And Hell

A. "By heaven, we mean eternal life in our enjoyment of God; by hell, we mean eternal death in our rejection of God." (3) (question 116)

B. The Nicene Creed says, "We look for the resurrection of the dead, and the life of the world to come." (6)

C. "...Episcopalians do not believe in a physical heaven or hell; these are 'states of being.' (quote of W. Norman Pittenger)" (8)

D. "In 1996...the doctrinal commission of the Church of England said hell is not a place of fire and eternal torment." (5) (pg 7)

E. Proof Texts: Revelation 20:11-12, 15, 21:1-3

THE ANGLICAN AND EPISCOPAL CHURCHES REPRESENT THAT HOLY BAPTISM AND HOLY EUCHARIST FORGIVE SINS AND MOST LEADERS QUESTION THE VIRGIN BIRTH AND DEITY OF CHRIST MAKING THIS A FALSE RELIGION.

(1) Roman Catholic Church in England and Wales, https://www.liquisearch.com/roman catholic_church_in_england_and_wales#:~:text=England%20adhered%20to%20the%20Catholic%20Church%2(%20declaring%20himself%20Supreme%20Head.

(2) Episcopal Church in the United States of America, History, https://en.wikipedia.org /wiki/ Episcopal_Church_(United_States)

(3) Concerning The Catechism, Book of Common Prayer, 1979, Episcopal (USA), pages 843-862, http://anglicansonline.org/basics/catechism.html

(4) The Thirty-Nine Articles of Religion USA, Book of Common Prayer, 1979, Episcopal (USA), pages 867-876, http://www.bible.ca/cr-Anglican#us

(5) Protestant Denominations Today, David W. Cloud, Way Of Life Literature, Port Huron, MI, 2014

(6) The Nicene Creed, Book of Common Prayer, 1979, Episcopal (USA), page 529 http://anglicansonline.org/basics/nicene.html

(7) Church of England Clergy Doesn't Believe in the Physical Resurrection https://www.worldanglican.com/articles/church-of-england-clergy-doesn-t-believe-in-the-physical-resurrection-949

(8) Religions Of America, Leo Rosten, Simon and Schuster, 1975, page 103

DENOMINATIONS-Lesson 11

First Church of Christ Scientist (Christian Science)

I **Timothy 6:20-21**

Origin: Mary Baker Patterson (later Eddy) "...slipped on an icy sidewalk and was painfully injured. She later claimed that that this injury had been proclaimed fatal by her doctor. Three days later she picked up her Bible, opened it to Matthew 9:2-8 and read the account where Jesus healed the paralytic. At that point, she reported the healing truth dawned upon her, and she got up, fully cured." (1) (pg 144) "...Mary Baker Eddy always maintained that the date of her healing (February 1866) marked the beginning of Christian Science. She said this date coincided with the Second Coming of Christ. This event was spiritual and invisible...By 1870, Mary was teaching her system (twelve lessons for only $300)...In 1875, Mary finished writing *Science And Health*...The Church Of Christ (Scientist) *was* incorporated on August 23, 1879. The headquarters were set up in Boston...Mrs. Eddy was the church's first pastor and dominated its leadership until her death." (1) (pg 145)

Doctrinal Beliefs:

1. The Bible

A. "...the thirty thousand different readings in the Old Testament, and the three hundred thousand in the New, these facts show how a mortal and material sense stole into the divine record, with its own hue darkening to some extent the inspired pages. But mistakes could neither wholly obscure the divine Science of the Scriptures seen from Genesis to Revelation..." (2) (pg 139)

B. "Mrs. Eddy claimed...that a Christian Scientist should use her book as a textbook because God was its author." (1) (pg 146)

C. "No human pen nor tongue taught me the Science contained in this book, Science and Health..." (2) (pg 110)

D. "The Bible and *Science and Health* are considered the dual and impersonal pastor of the Church." (3) (Church Practices)

E. Proof texts: <u>Matthew 5:17-18</u>, <u>Proverbs 30:6</u>

2. Salvation

A. "Man is incapable of sin..." (2) (pg 475)

B. "...she says, man is not sinful; his birth and death are just illusions, and because God is in everything, man is just like God." (1) (pg 148)

C. "A request that God will save us is not all that is required." (2) (pg 2) "Prayer is not to be used as a confessional to cancel sin." (2) (pg 5)

D. "The material blood of Jesus was no more efficacious to cleanse from sin when it was shed on 'the accursed tree', than when it was flowing in his veins as he went daily about his Father's business." (1) (pg 150) "One sacrifice, however great, is insufficient to pay the debt of sin." (2) (pg 23)

E. "His (Jesus')...example was for the salvation of us all, but only through doing the works which he did and taught others to do." (2) (pg 51)

F. Proof Texts: <u>Romans 3:23, 10:13</u>, <u>Matthew 26:28</u>

3. Baptism

A. "BAPTISM. Purification by Spirit; submergence in Spirit." (2) (pg 581)

B. "Although they engage in some of the traditional Christian sacraments, they interpret them differently. Baptism is regarded as the continual purification of thought and deed." (3) (Church Practices)

C. Proof Text: <u>Acts 8:38-39</u>

4. The Church

A. "Christian Science is a Christian denomination...founded...with this purpose... *to...reinstate primitive Christianity and its lost element of healing.*"

(from the *Manual of The Mother Church* by Mary Baker Eddy) (3) (Church Beliefs)

B. "There is no ordained clergy in the Church. Services are conducted by Readers who read from the Bible, from 'Science and Health' and from lesson-sermons sent from the Mother Church...Lay Christian Science practitioners are trained in Church principles and present a prayer-based healing ministry to members and the public as an alternative to conventional medical services." (3) (Church Practices)

C. "Authority is vested in a Board of Directors who conduct The Mother Church business. It is composed of five members who hold their positions for an undefined interval and select their own successors." (3) (Church Practices)

D. Proof text: <u>Acts 20:28</u>

5. Jesus Christ

A. "...Jesus Christ is not God..." (2) (pg 361)

B. "The Virgin-mother conceived this idea of God, and gave to her ideal the name of Jesus..." (2) (pg 29) "Jesus was the offspring of Mary's self-conscious communion with God." (2) (pg 29-30)

C. "Jesus explained his cures, which appeared miraculous..." (2) (pg 138) "...the so-called miracles of Jesus..." (2) (pg 123) "Jesus restored Lazarus by the understanding that Lazarus had never died, not by an admission that his body had died and then lived again." (2) (pg 75)

D. "His disciples believed Jesus to be dead while he was hidden in the sepulcher, whereas he was alive..." (2) (pg 44) "...they saw him after his crucifixion and learned that he had not died." (1) (pg 149)

E. Proof texts: <u>John 11:14</u>, <u>I Corinthians 15:3-4</u>, <u>Colossians 2:9</u>

6. The Trinity (Godhead)

A. "The Jewish tribal Jehovah was a man-projected God, liable to wrath, repentance, and human changeableness (S & H, 140)." (4) (pg 116)

B. "God is understood as the all-loving, omnipotent Father-Mother, and Christ Jesus as His Son.." (3) (Church Beliefs)

C. "Life, Truth, and Love constitute the triune Person called God...in office: God the Father-Mother; Christ the spiritual idea of sonship; divine Science or the Holy Comforter." (2) (pg 331)

D. Proof Texts: I John 5:7, I Peter 1:2

7. Heaven And Hell

A. "The sinner makes his own hell by doing evil, and the saint his own heaven by doing right." (2) (pg 266)

B. "the olden opinion that hell is fire and brimstone, has yielded somewhat to the metaphysical fact that suffering is a thing of mortal mind instead of body; so, in place of material flames and odor, mental anguish is generally accepted as the penalty for sin. (Miscellaneous Writings, page 237)" (4) (pg 123)

C. "No final judgment awaits mortals, for the judgment-day of wisdom comes hourly and continually..." (2) (pg 291)

D. Proof Texts: Luke 16: 22-23

CHRISTIAN SCIENCE HAS NOTHING "CHRISTIAN" ABOUT IT! THIS RELIGION IS DEFINITELY A FALSE DENOMINATION THAT STATES FLATLY THAT "JESUS CHRIST IS NOT GOD" AND THAT A PERSON IS SAVED ONLY BY DOING THE WORKS OF CHRISTIAN SCIENCE!

---

(1) So What's The Difference?, Fritz Ridenour, Regal Books Division, G/L Publications, Glendale, California, 1967, 1968, 1969, 1970.

(2) Science and Health with Key to the Scriptures, Mary Baker G. Eddy, Published by the Trustees under her Will, Boston, U.S.A., Copyright renewed 1934.

(3) The Church of Christ, Scientist (Christian Science), Church Practices,

http://www.religioustolerance.org/cr_sci.htm

(4) <u>The Kingdom of the Cults</u>, Walter Martin, Bethany Fellowship, Inc., Minneapolis, Minnesota, 1965, 1977.

DENOMINATIONS-Lesson 12

Hindu

Origin: "Hinduism is called (*Sanatana Dharma*-the eternal religion). The classical theory of the origins of Hinduism traces the religion's roots to the Indus valley civilization circa 4000 to 2200 BCE." (1) Through history there arose four principal Hindu denominations–Saivism, Shaktism, Vaishnavism and Smartism. (2) (Question 1) There are more than 1.2 billion Hindus in the world today, mostly in India and Nepal. Hindus numbered 1.2 million in the United States in 2004.

Doctrinal Beliefs:

1. The Bible

A. "Our 'Bible' is called the *Veda*. The *Veda*, which means 'wisdom', is comprised of four ancient and holy scriptures which all Hindus revere as the revealed word of God." (2) (Question 7)

B. "The primary sacred texts of Hinduism are the *Vedas*: the *Rig Veda, Sama Veda, Yajur Veda and Atharva Veda*. The *Vedas* contain hymns, incantations, and rituals from ancient India...Estimates of its date of composition in oral form range from 1500 BCE to 4000 BCE...The date when the *Vedas* were placed in written form is unknown. Various dates from 600 to after 300 BCE have been suggested." (1)

C. "1. I believe in the divinity of the Vedas, the world's most ancient scripture, and venerate the Ågamas as equally revealed. These primordial hymns are God's word..." (3) ("nine beliefs of Hinduism")

D. I found no quotes from the Bible, only from their scriptures and gurus.

E. Proof texts: <u>Matthew 15:9</u>, <u>Isaiah 34:16</u>

2. Salvation

A. "5. I believe that the soul reincarnates, evolving through many births until all *karmas* have been resolved, and *moksha* (spiritual knowledge and liberation from the cycle of rebirth) is attained. Not a single soul will be eternally deprived of this destiny" (3) ("nine beliefs of Hinduism")

B. "I myself have had many lives before this one and expect to have more. Finally, when I have it all worked out and all the lessons have been learned, I will attain enlightenment and moksha, liberation. This means I will still exist, but will no longer be pulled back to be born in a physical body." (2) (Question 2)

C. "9. I believe that no particular religion teaches the only way to salvation above all others, but that all genuine religious paths are facets of God's Pure Love and Light, deserving tolerance and understanding." (3) ("nine beliefs of Hinduism")

D. Proof texts: <u>John 14:6</u>, <u>Titus 3:5</u>

3. Baptism

A. "The *Namakarana Samskara*, Hindu Name-Giving Sacrament, represents the formal entrance into the Hindu religion - the equivalent of the sacrament of Baptism in the Christian faith. Like Baptism in the West, the *Namakarana Samskara* is usually given to a child, around the tenth day following birth. However, for those who are born in the West, or outside of Hinduism, and who later through reflection and belief convert to this most ancient religion, the sacrament can be received as an adult." (4)

B. Proof Texts: <u>Matthew 28:18-20</u>, <u>Acts 8:12</u>

4. The Church

A. "It is in the Hindu temple that...devotees invoke the Gods of our religion. The temple is built as a palace in which the Gods live. It is the home of the Gods, a sacred place unlike every other place on the earth...The physical representation of the God, be it a stone or metal image, a yantra or other sacred form, simply marks the place that the God will manifest in or hover over in his etheric body." (5) (Communicating with God and the gods)

B. "Hindus do not worship a stone or metal 'idol' as God. We worship God through the image...The stone or metal deity images in Hindu temples and shrines are not mere symbols of the Gods. They are the form through which their love, power and blessings flood forth into this world. " (2) (Question 5)

C. 7. "I believe that a spiritually awakened master, or *satguru*, is essential to know the Transcendent Absolute..." (3) ("nine beliefs of Hinduism")

D. Proof texts: <u>Romans 1:23, 25</u>, <u>Ephesians 4:11-12</u>, <u>I Timothy 2:5</u>

5. Jesus Christ

A. "Hindus say the teenage Jesus traveled across Southeast Asia, learning yogic traditions and returning home to be a guru to the Jews. To Hindus, Jesus' proclamation 'The Father and I are one' confirmed the Hindu idea that everyone, through rigorous spiritual practice, can realize his own universal 'god-consciousness.'" (6)

B. "Hindus believe...Christ is just one of many incarnations, or sons of God. Christ is not **the** Son of God. He was no more divine than any other man and He did not die for man's sins." (7) (pg103)

C. Proof texts: <u>Matthew 16:16-17</u>, <u>Hebrews 1:1-3</u>

6. The Trinity (Godhead)

A. 2. "I believe in a one, all-pervasive Supreme Being who is immanent and transcendent, both Creator and Unmanifest Reality. 6. I believe that divine beings exist in unseen worlds and that temple worship, rituals, sacraments as well as personal devotionals create a communion with these devas and Gods." (3) ("nine beliefs of Hinduism")

B. "In the Hindu pantheon there are said to be 333 million Gods. Hindus believe in one Supreme Being. The plurality of Gods are perceived as divine creations of that one Being. (Brahman)" (5) (A Hierarchy Of Gods Guide Hinduism)

C. "Some view Hinduism as Trinitarian because *Brahman* is simultaneously visualized as a triad—one God with three persons: *Brahma* the Creator... *Vishnu, (Krishna)* the Preserver...*Shiva*, the Destroyer..." (1)

D. Proof Texts: <u>Exodus 20:1-6</u>, <u>Psalm 135:5, 15-18</u>

7. Heaven And Hell

A. Dr. S. Radhakrishnan, renowned philosopher and president of India from 1962 to 1967, wrote: "There is no Hell, for that means there is a place where God is not, and there are sins which exceed his love." (8)

B. "...the soul (*Atman*) can be united with the ultimate truth (*Brahman*) through contemplation and mediation ." (1) "...it is said to have passed into *Nirvana*" (8) (pg 96)

C. "Once physical births have ceased, this soul body still continues to evolve in subtle realms of existence. This effulgent body of the illumined soul, even after *Nirvikalpa Samadhi*, God-Realization, continues to evolve in the inner worlds until the final merger into Brahman." (5) (A Hierarchy Of Gods Guide Hinduism)

D. "It is a positive religion. There is no fear of fire and brimstone, hell or damnation to encourage the listeners to fear divine wrath and punishment.." (9)

E. Proof texts: <u>Matthew 5:22</u>, <u>10:28</u>, <u>18:9</u>, <u>23:33</u>, <u>Hebrews 9:27</u>

HINDUISM IS DEFINIELY A FALSE DENOMINATION BECAUSE OF A FALSE DOCTRINE OF JESUS CHRIST AND A WORKS AND MEDITATION BASED SALVATION.

---

(1) <u>Hinduism-A General Introduction</u>, http://www.religioustolerance.org/hinduism2.htm

(2) <u>Ten Questions People Ask About Hinduism...and ten terrific answers</u> https://www.hinduismtoday.com/magazine/april-may-june-2004/2004-04-ten-questions-people-ask-about-hinduism-and-ten-terrific-answers/

(3)   Nâmakarana   Saṃskâra,   Hindu   Name-Giving   Sacrament   Certificate, https://www.hinduismtoday.com/wpcontent/uploads/2021/03/NamakaranaCertLarge.pdf

(4) Baptism, July 20, 2005, in The Hinduism Forum, https://www.indiadivine.org/content/topic/971955-baptism/

(5)   God   and   Gods   of   Hinduism,https://www.himalayanacademy.com/readlearn/basics/god-and-gods-of-hinduism.

(6)What Do Hindus Believe About Jesus?, https://www.beliefnet.com/faiths/hinduism/ 2002/05/what-do-hindus-believe-about-jesus.aspx

(7) So What's the Difference?, Fritz Ridenour, Regal Books Division, G/L Publications, Glendale, California, 1969-1970.

(8)Hindu Wisdom, http://www.hinduwisdom.info/quotes21_40.htm

(9) Introduction To Hinduism, http://www.hinduwisdom.info/introduction_to_hinduism. htm

DENOMINATIONS-Lesson 13

Jehovah's Witnesses

I John 9-11

Origin: Charles Taze Russell, an 18 year old former Congregationalist, started a Bible study in Pittsburgh, Pennsylvania in 1870. In 1874 this group elected him "Pastor". His teachings centered around denial of eternal torment and rejecting "organized religion". In 1884 "Zion's Watch Tower Tract Society" was chartered (changed to "The Watch Tower Bible and Tract Society" in 1896). Headquarters were moved to Brooklyn, New York in 1908. They claim that "...in 1914...Jesus Christ was enthroned as king in the heavens." (1) (pg 94); "...the Devil was ousted from heaven..." (1) (pg 100); and "The Bible clearly pin-points the generation alive in 1914 C.E. as the one that will yet witness the ushering in of Kingdom rule..." (2) (pg 165). Russell died in 1916 and Joseph Franklin (Judge) Rutherford assumed leadership. In 1931 the name "Jehovah's Witnesses" was adopted. They published the <u>New World Translation of the Holy Scriptures</u> in 1960, with revisions in 1961, 1970 and 1984. Worldwide membership in 2021 was 87 million.

Doctrinal Beliefs:

1. The Bible

A. "...the translation committee of the Watch Tower (whose names were not released) cleverly claims for itself and its translation a peculiar freedom from what they define as 'the misleading influence of religious traditions which have their roots in paganism'. This 'influence', the Watch Tower insists, has colored the inspired Word of God...in all translations from John Wycliffe (1380) to the Revised Standard Version (1901)." (3) (pg 63)

B. "Although some 40 human 'secretaries' were used to record the Bible, Jehovah himself is its author." (4) (pg 20)

C. The New World Translation contains the name "Jehovah" 6973 times in the Old Testament and 237 times in the New Testament according to appendix 1 of its 1984 revision. The King James Version has the name "Jehovah" 7 times in the Old Testament only. One of them is wrong!

D. Exodus 6:2-3 in the N.W.T. says: "And God went on to speak to Moses and to say to him: 'I am Jehovah. And I used to appear to Abraham, Isaac and Jacob as God Almighty, but as respects my name Jehovah I did not make myself known to them.'" But, in the N.W.T., Genesis 12:8, 15:2, 18:3, 27, 30, 31, 32 Abraham calls God "Jehovah". Isaac Genesis 25:21 and Jacob Genesis 28:13 also knew God as "Jehovah" according to the N.W.T.! (The N.W.T. contradicts itself and adds "Jehovah" over 7000 times!)

E. The New World Translation; translated by Jehovah's Witnesses for Jehovah's Witnesses is unreliable and tainted by their false doctrines!

F. Proof texts: Psalms 119:89, Proverbs 30:6

2. Salvation

A. "...man does not have an immortal soul..." (2) (pg 43)

B. "For over 1,900 years there was a gathering together of the 'little flock' of 144,000 Christians...already ruling with Christ in heaven...Jesus said: 'I have other sheep'...A 'great crowd' of 'other sheep' are now being gathered. They will make up the first ones of the 'new earth'. Jehovah will protect them through 'the great tribulation' at the end of this wicked system to live on into the earthly paradise." (5) (pg 163-164)

C. "The thing to do now is to start to learn what God requires of you, to take in the vital knowledge contained in his Word, and then to act in harmony with it. This is the way that leads to eternal life...everlasting life in God's righteous new order." (2) (pg 189-190) (Physical life in Christ's Kingdom on earth)

D. "...a person could fall away and be judged unfavorably either now, or at Armageddon, or during the thousand years of Christ's reign, or at the end of the final test...into everlasting destruction. From Paradise Lost to Paradise Regained, page 241" (3) (pg 48)

E. Proof texts: Genesis 2:7, I Thessalonians 5:23, 1 Peter 1:5

3. Baptism

A. "...water baptism is a public demonstration that a person has dedicated his life to Jehovah and is presenting himself to do His will...water baptism is an important requirement..." (5) (pg 252)

B. "those who dedicate themselves to Jehovah on the basis of faith in the resurrected Christ, who get baptized in symbol of that and who then proceed to do God's will for his servants in our day are saved..." (4) (pg 100) (Baptism and continuing to do God's will are required for salvation!)

C. Proof Text: <u>Acts 8:12</u>

4. The Church

A. "For 1,545 years...Israel was the congregation of God. But they failed...So Jehovah brought into existence a new congregation, with which he made a new covenant. This congregation is identified in the Scriptures as the 'bride' of Christ...144,000 chosen by God to be...with his Son in heaven." (4) (pg 117)

B. "...the 'church of the firstborn who are written in the heavens'...are limited in number to 144,000." (1) (pg 115)

C. "Each year on Nisan 14, after sundown, the anointed followers of Jesus Christ in all parts of the earth commemorate his death...The 'other sheep' also attend, not as partakers of the bread and wine, but as respectful observers." (4) (pg 114)

D. "...the Governing Body is made up of spirit-anointed brothers from various lands...All their local congregations work in close cooperation with it. They look to the Governing Body to provide for appointment of elders and ministerial servants to care for the smooth functioning of the congregations." (4) (pg 121)

E. Proof texts: <u>Philippians 1:1</u>, <u>Revelation 7:4-8</u>

5. Jesus Christ

A. "Jesus...he is God's 'firstborn' Son. This means that he was created before the other sons of God's family. He is also God's 'only-begotten' Son, in that he is the only one directly created by Jehovah God." (1) (pg 47)

B. "Jesus was the equal of the perfect man Adam." (5) (pg 63)

C. "Jehovah God did not leave his Son dead in the grave, but raised him to life on the third day...But he was 'made alive in the spirit'...he appeared visibly to his disciples...in materialized bodies..." (1) (pg 52) (NOT a physical body)

D. They do not use B.C. or A.D. for dates, but B.C.E. and C.E.

E. Proof texts: John 1:1-3, John 10:17-18

6. The Trinity (Godhead)

A. "There is one solitary being from all eternity, Jehovah God, the Creator and Preserver of the Universe and of all things visible and invisible." (3)(pg 46)

B. "As for the 'Holy Spirit', the so-called third Person of the Trinity, we have already seen that this is not a person, but God's active force." (5) (pg 40)

C. "Even after his death and resurrection and ascension to heaven, Jesus was still not equal to his Father...Jesus is not Almighty God." (5) (pg 39-40)

D. Proof Texts: John 5:18, I John 5:7, Colossians 2:9

7. Heaven And Hell

A. "Those who follow Jesus Christ faithful to the death will inherit the heavenly Kingdom with Him. Men of good will who accept Jehovah and His Theocratic Rule will enjoy the 'new earth'; all others who reject Jehovah will be annihilated." (3) (pg 48)

B. "...hell, mankind's common grave, will be emptied of its unconscious dead. Some receive a resurrection to heavenly glory as spirit creatures, even as did Jesus Christ. However, the vast majority of mankind will be brought back to enjoy life on a restored earthly paradise. (1) (pg 45)

C. "...no soul or spirit separates from the body at death and continues conscious existence. Hence, there is no Scriptural foundation for the doctrine of eternal torment after death..." (2) (pg 90-91)

D. "(Gehenna)...The 'lake of fire' mentioned in Revelation...not conscious torment, but 'second death,' everlasting death or destruction. It is evident that this 'lake' is a symbol..." (1) (pg 44)

E. Proof texts: <u>Revelation 14:10-11, 19:20, 20:10, 21:8</u>

This group is DEFINITELY A FALSE RELIGION with incorrect doctrines about Jesus Christ AS A CREATED BEING and salvation BY WORKS.

---

(1) <u>The Truth That Leads to Eternal Life</u>, Watch Tower Bible and Tract Society of New York, 1968.

(2) <u>Is This Life All There Is?</u>, Watch Tower Bible and Tract Society of New York, 1974.

(3) <u>The Kingdom of the Cults</u>, Walter Martin, Bethany Fellowship, Inc., Minneapolis, Minnesota, 1965, 1977.

(4) <u>United in Worship of the Only True God</u>, Watch Tower Bible and Tract Society of New York, 1983.

(5) <u>You Can Live Forever in Paradise on Earth</u>, Watch Tower Bible and Tract Society of New York, 1982.

DENOMINATIONS-Lesson 14

Judaism

R<u>omans 9:1-5</u>

Origin: "Judaism: World religion that traces its origins to God's call to Abram (Abraham) to be the father of a great people who would inherit the land of Canaan and be the means of blessing to all mankind (Genesis 12). That people is identified as the children of Abraham's grandson, Jacob, who was renamed Israel. The foundation of Judaism is...the giving of the Law through Moses. The Israelites returned to the promised land of Canaan and became a small but powerful nation...the Jerusalem temple was destroyed, and the Jewish nation scattered (AD 70). What is now known as the religion of Judaism originated after AD 70...There are three main branches of modern Judaism: <u>Orthodox</u> (traditional, literal adherence to the Torah as interpreted by the Talmud), <u>Conservative</u> (a middle position advocating traditional beliefs and practices up to a point), and <u>Reform</u> (liberal, non-literal stance on the Torah and Talmud; often non-religious or secular with emphasis on Jewish culture)." (1) Approximately 5 million of the world's 13 million Jews live in the U. S.

Doctrinal Beliefs:

1. The Bible

A. "Judaism rests on two pillars. One is the Hebrew Bible, particularly the Pentateuch, or the five books of Moses, known as the Torah. It is the revelation of God, divine in origin and containing the earliest written laws and traditions of the Jewish people. The other pillar is the Talmud, a rabbinic commentary and enlargement of the Torah. It is an elaborate, discursive compendium that contains the written and oral laws of the faith." (2) (Page 6)

B. "The Talmud tells us (Tractate Makkot 23b) that there are 613 commandments (mitzvot) in the Torah; 248 Positive Commandments (do's) and 365 Negative Commandments (do not's). However, the Talmud does not provide us with a list of these commandments. (3) (The 613 Commandments (Mitzvot))

C. Proof texts: <u>Deuteronomy 4:2, 12:32, Matthew 15:1-9</u>

2. Salvation

A "...if you're worried about going to heaven, Jewish belief is that all good people have a share in the World to Come, as long as they connect their lives to the oneness of G-d and keep the Seven Laws of Noah." (4)

B. "The Seven Laws Of Noah: Embrace G-d's Oneness, Do Not Curse Him, Guard Human Life, Respect Animal Life, Respect the Property of Others, Live a Moral Family Life, Ensure Justice" (5)

C. "Rosh ha-Shanah Day...Teach us, O God, to labor for righteousness, and inscribe us in the Book of life." (6) (RH Day Virtual Prayer Book)

D. Proof Text: <u>Romans 10:1-3</u>

3. Baptism

A. "Males <u>were</u> admitted into Judaism by circumcision, females by a free-will offering; after Christ, the Jews added baptism for both sexes admitted into their faith...Proselyte Baptism is...an imitation of the Christian rite, incorporated into Judaism after the Destruction of Jerusalem, A. D. 70." (7) (pg 30-31)

B. "Although the term "baptism" is not used to describe the Jewish rituals, the purification rites in Halakha, Jewish law and tradition, called tvilah, have some similarity to baptism, and the two have been linked. The tvilah is the act of immersion in naturally-sourced water, called a mikva. In the past Hebrew Bible and other Jewish texts, immersion in water for ritual purification... Immersion is required for converts to Judaism. Immersion in the mikvah represents a change in status in regards to purification, restoration, and qualification for full religious participation" (8) (Background in Jewish ritual)

C. Proof texts: <u>Acts 2:41, 8:12</u>

---

1. https://www.chabad.org/library/article_cdo/aid/433240/jewish/God.htm

4. The Church

A. "The Sabbath is the most important day in the Jewish calendar. It begins each Friday evening at sunset and comes to an end late on Saturday evening. The Sabbath symbolizes the original seventh day on which God rested after completing the creation of the universe. Work is not permitted and there are statutory religious services. There are three *'pilgrim'* festivals each year...These were the Passover...the Feast of Weeks...and the Feast of Tabernacles...Other festivals are Lag B'Omer, Hanukkah, Purim, Tish B'av, Rosh Hosanah, Yom Kippur, Simkat Torah." (2) (pg 22)

B. "A synagogue (שׁוּל) (*shul*) is a place of Jewish worship. In addition to housing a sanctuary for services, synagogues serve as the centerpoint of Jewish life. Known in Hebrew as beit *knesset* (בֵּית כְּנֶסֶת), "house of gathering," the synagogue can be found virtually wherever there are Jews and has been in use since the Babylonian exile." (3) (The Synagogue (Shul))

C. Proof texts: <u>Colossians 1:18</u>, <u>Ephesian 5:23</u>

5. Jesus Christ

A. "There is no role for Jesus in the theological scheme of Judaism...to claim that He was the Messiah is to run counter to Jewish understanding of what *messiah* means." (2) (pg 20)

B. "In the first century AD, Christianity originated with the belief that Jesus was that promised Messiah. The Jewish establishment at that time, however, rejected Jesus' claim to be the Messiah..." (1)

C. Proof Text: <u>John 10:30-33</u>

6. The Trinity (Godhead)

A. "The first Fundamental tenet of Judaism is the existence of one supreme deity. God is One, omnipotent, omniscient, and without limitation or form. He is the Creator, the Master of the universe as well as an active participant in human affairs...Twice daily a devout Jew recites the *Shema*...'Hear, O Israel: the Lord our God is one Lord...'" (2) (pg 17)

B. What they believe about Jesus: "The claim that He is in some sense God is blasphemy..." (2) (pg 20)

C. Proof Texts: <u>I John 5:7</u>, <u>II Corinthians 13:14</u>

7. Heaven And Hell

A. "...because Judaism is primarily focused on life here and now rather than on the afterlife, Judaism does not have much dogma about the afterlife, and leaves a great deal of room for personal opinion. It is possible for an Orthodox Jew to believe that the souls of the righteous dead go to a place similar to the Christian heaven, or that they are reincarnated through many lifetimes, or that they simply wait until the coming of the messiah, when they will be resurrected. Likewise, Orthodox Jews can believe that the souls of the wicked are tormented by demons of their own creation, or that wicked souls are simply destroyed at death, ceasing to exist. (9)

B. Proof Texts: <u>Psalm 9:17</u>, <u>Luke 16:22-24</u>

ALTHOUGH WE OWE MUCH TO THE JEWS, <u>PRESENT</u> JUDAISM, WITH AN INCOR-RECT DOCTRINE OF JESUS CHRIST AND SALVATION BY WORKS IS A FALSE RELIGION.

---

(1) <u>Index of Cults and Religions: Judaism</u>, http://www.watchman.org/index-of-cults-and-religions/#J

(2) <u>Three Monotheistic Faiths - Judaism, Christianity, Islam:</u> Andrea C. Paterson[2], AuthorHouse,2009,https://books.google.com/
books?id=tuuys4HxSzcC&printsec=frontcover#v=onepage&q&f=false

(3) <u>Jewish Practice</u>, https://www.chabad.org/library/article_cdo/aid/1675888/jewish/
Jewish-Practice.htm

(4) <u>Should I convert to Judaism?</u>, https://www.chabad.org/library/article_cdo/aid/857823/jewish/
Should-I-Convert-to-Judaism.htm

(5) <u>The Seven Laws Of Noah</u>, https://www.chabad.org/library/article_cdo/aid/5559665/jewish/
The-Seven-Laws-of-Noah.htm

(6) <u>RH day virtual prayerbook</u>, https://www.etzhaim.org/wp-content/uploads/2020/09/RH-day-
virtual-prayerbook.pdf

---

2. https://www.google.com/search?tbo=p&tbm=bks&q=inauthor:%22Andrea+C.+Paterson%22

(7) The History of the Baptists, Thomas Armitage, Morningside Publishing Co., Chicago, 1887, Reprinted, Baptist Bible College, Springfield, Mo, 1977.

(8) History of Baptism, https://en.wikipedia.org/wiki/History_of_baptism#Background_in_Jewish_ritual

(9) Olam Ha-Ba: The Afterlife, http://www.jewfaq.org/olamhaba.htm

DENOMINATIONS-Lesson 15

Kabbalah

Colossians 2:8, Titus 1:14

Origin: "With regard to the author and origin of the Kabbalah, I cannot do better that give the following extract from Dr. Ginsburg's 'Essay on the Kabbalah'...The Kabbalah was first taught by God himself to a select company of angels...in Paradise. After the Fall the angels...communicated this...to the disobedient child of earth...From Adam it passed over to Noah...Abraham...who emigrated with it to Egypt...the Egyptians obtained some knowledge of it...Moses...was initiated into the Kabbalah in the land of his birth...but received lessons in it from one of the angels...He covertly laid down the principles of this secret doctrine in the first four books of the Pentateuch...and initiated the seventy elders into the secrets...David and Solomon were...deeply initiated into the Kabbalah. No one, however, dared to write it down, till Schimeon Ben Yochai, who lived at the time of the destruction of the second temple...the celebrated work called ZHR, *Zohar*, splendor, which is the grand storehouse of Kabbalism." (1) (pg 4, 6-7) "It is considered an esoteric off-branch of Judaism because it teaches meditation, loyalties, and mystical enhancements to a select few. It originated for Jews only, but many non-Jews have studied Kabbalah for the last 500 years." (2) "As well as Madonna, other celebrities that have followed Kabbalah include Ashton Kutcher and ex-wife Demi Moore, Lindsay Lohan, Monica Lewinsky, Ariana Grande, James Van Der Beek and Donald Trump's ex-wife Marla Maples. Other celebrities who have been associated with the religion include Britney Spears, Mick Jagger, Naomi Campbell, Mary-Kate Olsen, Paris Hilton and Elizabeth Taylor." (3)

Doctrinal Beliefs:

1. The Bible

A. "The Old Testament, and in particular the Five Books of Moses, is at the core of the Zohar." (1) (FOREWORD pg vi)

B. "the *Zohar* is the instrument we use to help us to decode the Bible, which was never meant to be taken literally." (5)

C. "The Bible...contains numberless obscure and mysterious passages which are utterly unintelligible without some key wherewith to unlock their meaning. THAT KEY IS GIVEN IN THE KABBALAH." (1) (Pg 1)

D. "...each letter has its own peculiar numerical value, and from this circumstance results the important fact that every word is a number and every number is a word." (1) (pg 3) "...every letter of a word is taken for the initial or abbreviation of another word, so that from the letters of a word a sentence may be formed." (1) (pg 9) "Besides all these rules, there are certain meanings hidden in the *shape* of the letters of the Hebrew alphabet..." (1) (pg 13)

E. Proof Texts: <u>Proverbs 30:6</u>, <u>Titus 1:14</u>, <u>II Peter 1:19-20</u>

2. Salvation

A. "The basic principle of Kabbalah is that the seeker pursues spiritual practice to transform his or her being and rise through the levels of worlds, to bring his or her own will back to the Divine will, while opening a way for the higher energies to flow down to this world, and thereby advancing the great process of tikkun olam...we discover a vision of unbounded meaning: perfecting ourselves[1], perfecting the world, and helping God." (6)

B. "Souls perfected on this earth pass on to another station." (1) (pg 52)

C. Proof Texts: <u>Genesis 2:7</u>, <u>Titus 3:5</u>

3. Baptism

A. See "Judaism" Lesson 14 for baptismal practices.

B. Proof Text: <u>Matthew 28:19-20</u>

4. The Church

---

1. http://www.innerfrontier.org/Practices/WhoAmI.htm

A. "...in the late 20th and early 21st centuries there has been a revival in interest in Kabbalah in all branches of liberal Judaism." (4) (Conservative, Reform and Reconstructionist Judaism)

B. "The startling truth is that Kabbalah was never meant for a specific sect. Rather, it was intended to be used by all humanity to unify the world...why so many people of different faiths become connected to Kabbalah is that it is a way of life that can enhance any religious practice. Christians, Hindus, Buddhists, Muslims, and Jews use Kabbalah to improve their spiritual experience." (8)

C. Proof Texts: <u>Colossians 1:18</u>, <u>Ephesians 5:25</u>

5. Jesus Christ

A. "Christianity teaches that the Messiah came as the Son of God (Jesus Christ) to redeem man from evil. Judaism teaches that the Messiah has yet to come and redeem Israel. Kabbalah's philosophy does not include the sinful nature of man, and therefore, there is no need of the redeeming qualities of a Messiah." (2) (Kabbalah vs. Christianity vs. Judaism)

B. "Jesus performed his miracles using kabbalistic techniques learned from the Essenes, a Jewish sect of that time that was involved in mysticism." (8)

C. "...we have returned to the very Kabbalah our predecessors scorned. The stone that the builders rejected has become the head cornerstone..." (4) (Conservative, Reform and Reconstructionist Judaism)

D. Proof Texts: <u>Romans 5:8</u>, <u>Acts 4:10-12</u>

6. The Trinity (Godhead)

A. "This true essence of G-d is known as Ein Sof, which literally means 'without end'...The Ein Sof interacts with the universe through ten emanations from this essence, known as the Ten Sefirot...The Ten Sefirot include both masculine and feminine qualities. Kabbalah pays a great deal of attention to the feminine aspects of G-d...The Sefirot are not separate deities...They are intimately a part of G-d." (8)

B. "Now we hear much of the Father and the Son, but we hear nothing of the Mother in the ordinary religions of the day. But in Kabbalah we find that the Ancient of Days conforms Himself simultaneously into the Father and the Mother, and thus begats the Son." (1) (pg 28) "...there is one trinity...it consists of the crown, the king and the queen. (In some senses this is the Christian Trinity of the Father, Son, and Holy Spirit..." (1) (pg36-37) "Crown; Father, King; Son, Queen; Spirit" (1) (pg48)

C. "Rabbi Yitzchak ben Sheshet Perfet, 1326-1408, stated that Kabbalah was 'worse than Christianity', as it made God into 10, not just into three." (9)

D. Proof Texts: <u>I John 5:7</u>, <u>John 14:16-17, 26</u>

7. Heaven And Hell

A. "The *Zohar* says that the first verse of *Mishpatim*: "These are the laws that you should put before them," refers to the law of reincarnation, indicating that the travel of the soul from one lifetime to another does in fact exist...This has happened to all of us; we have, each one of us, come back because we did not recognize what was required of us in a past lifetime...the cause of our current experience, good or bad, is in all likelihood not linked to anything we have done today; it could be something we did 40 lifetimes in the past." (5)

B. "...the abode of darkness...seven Hells occupied by those demons which represent incarnate human vices, and torture those who have given themselves up to such vices in earth-life." (1) (pg 40)

C. Proof Text: <u>Luke 16:22-23</u>

KABBALAH IS DEFINITELY A FALSE RELIGION WITH INCORRECT DOCTRINES OF SALVATION AND JESUS CHRIST!

---

(1) <u>The Kabbalah, The Essential Texts From The Zohar</u>, Watkins Publishing, 2006, Sixth Floor, Castle House, 75-76 Wells Street, London W1T 3QH

(2) <u>Kabbalah-What Is It?</u>, http://www.allaboutreligion.org/kabbalah.htm

(3) <u>Which celebrities followed Kabbalah?</u>, https://news.yahoo.com/kabbalah-religion-beloved-celebrities-noughties

(4) <u>Kabbalah History</u>, http://en.wikipedia.org/wiki/Kabbalah#Kabbalah:_History:

(5) <u>Reincarnation and Our Spiritual Work</u>, Rav Michael Laitman, PhD,https://www.kabbalah.com/en/articles/reincarnation-and-our-spiritual-work/

(6) <u>Tikkun Olam: The Spiritual Purpose of Life</u>, http://www.innerfrontier.org/Practices/TikkunOlam.htm

(7) <u>F. A. Q.</u>, The Kabbalah Centre, http://www.kabbalah.com/kabbalah/03.php

(8) <u>Kabbalah And Jewish Mysticism</u>, http://www.jewfaq.org/kabbalah.htm

(9) <u>Kabbalah - is it really legitimate for Jews?</u>, https://fightthenewage.blogspot.com/2013/11/kabbalah-is-it-really-legitimate-for.html

DENOMINATIONS-Lesson 16

Lutheran

<u>Colossians 2:8</u>

Origin: All Lutheran Churches trace their roots directly to the Protestant Reformation of the 1500's. Martin Luther (1483-1546), a German Roman Catholic priest, became aware of differences between the Bible and church practices. In 1517 he nailed his "95 Thesis" (which questioned many Roman Catholic doctrines) to the church door at Wittenberg University. Followers of Martin Luther's teachings were called "Lutherans" by their enemies and adopted the name themselves. Lutheran beliefs became widespread in Germany and the Scandinavian countries, later spreading throughout the world. The three largest Lutheran denominations in America are the Evangelical Lutheran Church in America (ELCA), the Lutheran Church - Missouri Synod (LCMS), and the Wisconsin Evangelical Lutheran Synod (WELS). All three groups accept the <u>Book Of Concord</u> as the true declaration of their beliefs.

Doctrinal Beliefs:

1. The Bible

A. "The Lutheran Church—Missouri Synod accepts the Scriptures as the inspired and inerrant Word of God...We accept he Lutheran Confessions as articulated in the Book of Concord of 1580 because they are drawn from the Word of God, and on that account we regard their doctrinal content as a true and binding exposition of Holy Scripture..." (1) (Lutheran Confessions)

B. "The ELCA's official Confession of Faith identifies the Scriptures of the Old and New Testament...the Apostles', Nicene and Athanasian Creeds; and the Lutheran confessional writings in the Book of Concord as the basis for our teaching." (2) (Teaching, Scriptures, Creeds and Confessions)

C. In 7 sermons from 7 Churches which I copied from the internet, there were a total of 27 quotations from Scripture. This is an average of less than 4 per sermon and that includes the beginning text and references to it! Translations used were: N.I.V.(13), R.S.V.(3), N.R.S.V.(7), N.A.S.B.(4).

D. Having dealt with the N.W.T, N.R.S.V, C.E.V. and the N.I.V. in previous lessons, let's look at the New American Standard Bible. Ten references to Jesus as "Lord" are left out. Verses that teach the bodily resurrection, hell, prophecies fulfilled by Christ, the trinity, the deity of Christ, Jesus coming to save the lost, repentance, and salvation before baptism are altered, deleted or called into question by brackets around them and a footnote that says, "the best ancient manuscripts do not contain this verse".

E. Proof texts: <u>Colossians 1:2</u> ("and the Lord Jesus Christ" left out), <u>Mark 16:9-20</u> (twelve verses called into question about the resurrection, plus one verse maybe added?), <u>Luke 2:33</u> (changes "Joseph" to "His father").

2. Salvation

A. "Article IX. Of Baptism...they teach that it is necessary to salvation, and that through Baptism is offered the grace of God, and that children are to be baptized who, being offered to God through Baptism are received into God's grace. They condemn the Anabaptists, who reject the baptism of children, and say that children are saved without Baptism." (3) (The Augsburg Confession, 1530)

B. "The Sacrament of Holy Baptism. What gifts or benefit does Baptism bestow? It effects <u>forgiveness of sins</u>, delivers from death and the devil, and <u>grants eternal salvation</u>..." (3) (Small Catechism, Martin Luther, 1529)

C. "The Sacrament of the Altar. What is the Sacrament of the Altar? Instituted by Jesus Christ himself, <u>it is the true body and blood of our Lord Jesus Christ</u> ...given to us Christians to eat and drink." (3) (Small Catechism, Martin Luther, 1529) (This is called "transubstantiation" and is identical with Roman Catholic doctrine.)

D. Concerning eternal security: "ARTICLE XII: OF REPENTANCE. For those who have fallen after Baptism there is remission of sins whenever they are converted...They condemn the Anabaptists, who deny that those once justified can lose the Holy Ghost." (3) (Small Catechism, Martin Luther, 1529)

E. Proof Texts: I Corinthians 1:17-18, 11:24-25, Galatians 2:16

3. Baptism

A. "Therefore state it most simply thus, that the power, work, profit, fruit, and end of Baptism is this, namely, to save. For no one is baptized in order that he may become a prince, but, as the words declare, that he be saved..." (3) (The Large Catechism-Holy Baptism, Martin Luther, 1529)

B. Luther, speaking of baptism mentions, "...a handful of water...laver of regeneration...water to be poured upon you...the water, is sprinkled." (3) (The Large Catechism-Holy Baptism, Martin Luther, 1529) (He never mentions that immersion is the only Scriptural mode of baptism mentioned in the Bible.)

C. Proof texts: Mark 16:15-16, Matthew 3:16-17

4. The Church

A. The Evangelical Lutheran Church In America (ELCA) are now "Full Communion Partners" with Presbyterian Church (USA), Reformed Church In America, United Church Of Christ, Episcopal Church, Moravian Church and United Methodist Church. This involves accepting "each other as rightly preaching the Gospel", "mutual recognition of Baptism and a sharing of the Lord's Supper" and "recognizing each other's ordained ministers". (2) (Ecumenical-and-Inter- Religious-Relations/Full-Communion/History)

B. "As of 1993, the ELCA had 1,358 ordained women clergy." (4) (Pg 30)

C. "Our Churches...condemn Anabaptists" (our forefathers) five times in the Augsburg Confession. (3)

D. "In 1992 the ELCA Division for Church in Society authorized the distribution of a report on human sexuality which claims that 'homosexuals were created by God and that sexual relationships outside of marriage are not always wrong.' An ELCA youth program guide...teaches young people that the Bible does not condemn homosexuality." (4) (Pg 33)

E. Proof texts: <u>Revelation 1:10-11</u>, <u>I Timothy 2:12</u>, <u>Romans 1:26-28</u>

5. Jesus Christ

A. "The 2nd Article: Redemption. I believe in Jesus Christ, his only son, our Lord: who was conceived by the Holy Spirit, born of the Virgin Mary, suffered under Pontius Pilate, was crucified, dead, and buried; He descended into hell; the third day he rose from the dead; he ascended into heaven, and is seated on the right hand of God, the Father Almighty...." (3) (Small Catechism, Martin Luther, 1529)

B. "I might speak of the 'empty tomb' on Easter, but I would not have meant that I believed that Jesus actually, physically rose from the dead." (4) (Pg 32)

C. "For the ELCA, the doctrine of the virginal conception of Jesus seems an embarrassment, as if educated people can no longer believe such things Doubt is the prevailing mood as well...on resurrection...Still more seriously, the essay skirts the fact that Jesus rose bodily from the dead. His Easter appearances it calls 'apparitions' as if the disciples did not really see their Lord standing bodily before them." (5)

D. Proof Text: <u>I Timothy 2:5</u>, <u>Matthew 1:18-25</u>, <u>John 20:26-27</u>

6. The Trinity (Godhead)

A. "The three persons of the Trinity are coequal and coeternal, one God." (1)

B. Proof texts: <u>Hebrews 9:14</u>, <u>I Peter 1:2</u>

7. Heaven And Hell

A. "ARTICLE XVII: OF CHRIST'S RETURN TO JUDGMENT. At the consummation of the World Christ will appear for judgment and will raise up all the dead; He will give to the godly and elect eternal life and everlasting joys, but ungodly men and devils He will condemn to be tormented without end." (3) (The Augsburg Confession, 1530)

B. "OF THE MILLENNIUM...we reject every type of millennialism...that Christ will return visibly to this earth a thousand years before the end of the world...or that...a universal conversion...of Israel...will take place." (1) (Doctrines-Of The Millennium)

C. Proof Texts: <u>Revelation 20:4-6</u>, <u>Romans 11:25-27</u>

LUTHERANISM REQUIRES SACRAMENTS FOR SALVATION, MAKING IT A FALSE RELIGION! IN ADDITION, ECLA TEACHING EXPRESSES DOUBTS ABOUT THE VIRGIN BIRTH AND BODILY RESURRECTION OF CHRIST.

---

(1) <u>Lutheran Church—Missouri Synod: Beliefs and Practice</u>, adopted 1932, https://www.lcms.org/about/beliefs

(2) <u>Confession of Faith of the Evangelical Lutheran Church in America</u>, 1995, https://elca.org/Faith

(3) <u>Book Of Concord</u>, http://bookofconcord.org/

(4) <u>Protestant Denominations Today</u>, David W. Cloud, Way Of Life Literature, Port Huron, MI, 2014

(5) <u>What Is the ELCA Problem About?</u>, https://www.elcatoday.com/what-is-the-elca-problem-about.html

DENOMINATIONS-Lesson 17

Mennonite/Amish

I **I Thessalonians 3:14-15**

Origin: "Mennonites are Anabaptists...The first Anabaptists separated from the state church when they began re-baptizing adults and refusing to baptize infants until they could make an adult decision to follow Christ. Mennonites are named for Menno Simons[1] (1496-1561), a Dutch priest who embraced Anabaptist theology as an alternative to Catholicism" (1) "It cost something to be a Mennonite in those days. Many were burned at the stake, and the times were rare when they were entirely free from persecution. Menno himself was pursued with murderous fury, but the Lord preserved him in a remarkable way. His writings were spared and he was permitted to die a natural death." (2) "Mennonite Church USA (MC USA) is the largest Mennonite denomination in the United States with 16 conferences, approximately 530 congregations and 62,000 members...MC USA is part of Mennonite World Conference, a global faith family that includes churches in 86 countries...Mennonites and Amish are both Anabaptists and share common historical roots. While the groups agree on basic Christian doctrine, their differences come in interpreting how those practices should be lived out. (1) "The original difference in opinion came in 1693, when Jacob Ammann, a Swiss Anabaptist leader, felt that the church leaders were not holding to strict separation from the world and that spiritual renewal was needed. Ammann did not believe that the ban, or shunning, was being practiced as it should be. He separated from the Swiss Brethren segment of the Anabaptists over this issue and his followers were nicknamed "Amish." (1) "Total population 373,620 (2022, Old Order Amish)" (3)

Doctrinal Beliefs:

1. The Bible

---

1. https://gameo.org/index.php?title=Menno_Simons_(1496-1561)

A. "We believe that all Scripture is inspired by God through the Holy Spirit for instruction in salvation and training in righteousness...Scripture references are to the New Revised Standard Version (NRSV)." (4) (Article 4. Scripture)

B. There are 388 words of Jesus that are in the KJV, but are deleted from the NRSV! The NRSV leaves out 18 WHOLE VERSES that are in the KJV! Other changes in the NRSV: Isaiah 7:14 "virgin" to "young woman", Daniel 3:25 "the Son of God" to "the appearance of a god", John 6:69 "Christ, the Son of the living God" to "the Holy One of God", Romans 14:10 "Judgment seat of Christ" to "judgment seat of God", Ephesians 3:9 Deletes "by Jesus Christ" when God created. The KJV has 84 references to Him as "Lord Jesus Christ". The NRSV has only 62, a reduction of about 25%!

C. Proof texts: Psalms 12:6-7

2. Salvation

A. "We confess, that beginning with Adam and Eve, humanity has disobeyed God, given way to the tempter, and chosen to sin. All have fallen short of the Creator's intent..." (4) (Article 7. Sin)

B. "We believe that, through...Jesus Christ, God offers salvation from sin and a new way of life to all people. We receive God's salvation when we repent of sin and accept Jesus Christ as Savior and Lord." (4) (Article 8. Salvation)

C. "membership in the community and participation in its rites was the means to salvation...God did not grant salvation because of inner experience. Salvation came only by actual participation in Christ, by suffering, yielding, dying to self as he did...Amish are less concerned with achieving individual salvation through a personal belief in Jesus Christ. It's said that they regard any claim by an individual to be 'saved' as an expression of pride, and something to be avoided." (5)

D. "While Mennonites hold tightly to the belief that we are saved through God's powerful gift of grace, we don't subscribe to the "eternal security," or "once saved, always saved" theology... the individual may still choose to forfeit his/her right to salvation." (6)

E. Proof Texts: <u>Galatians 3:1-3</u>, <u>I John 5:11-13</u>

3. Baptism

A. "Baptism by water is a sign that a person has repented, received forgiveness, renounced evil, and died to sin, through the grace of God in Christ Jesus...The Church may baptize by pouring, immersion, or sprinkling of water...Infants and children have no need for baptism, since they are safe in the care of God." (4) (Article 11. Baptism)

B. Proof text: <u>Acts 8:35-39</u>

4. The Church

A. "We believe that the <u>church</u> is the assembly of those who have accepted God's offer of salvation through faith in Jesus Christ...The church exists as a community of believers in the local congregation, as a community of congregations, and as the worldwide community of faith." (4) (Article 9. The Church Of Jesus)

B. "Supportive Communities Network (SCN) is a program of the Brethren Mennonite Council for Lesbian, Gay, Bisexual, and Transgender Interests. It is a network of Mennonite and Church of the Brethren communities who are publicly affirming of gay, lesbian, transgender, and bisexual members." (7)

C. "The governing body of the largest Mennonite denomination in the United States passed a resolution on Sunday (May 29) confessing to 'committing violence against LGBTQ people' and committing to LGBTQ inclusion...In a separate vote, Mennonite Church USA also repealed instructions to pastors not to officiate at marriages between people of the same sex...Excluding LGBTQIA people from the church is a rejection of God's joyous delight in the diversity of creation..." (8)

D. Proof texts: <u>I Thessalonians 1:1</u>, <u>I Corinthians 6:9-11</u>

5. Jesus Christ

A. "We believe in <u>Jesus Christ</u>, The Word of God become flesh. He is the Savior of the world, who has...reconciled us to God by his death on a cross. He was declared to be Son of God by his resurrection from the dead. He is the head of the church...coming again to reign with God in glory." (4) (Article 2. Jesus Christ)

B. Proof Texts: <u>John 1:14</u>, <u>I Corinthians 15:1-4</u>

6. The Trinity (Godhead)

A. "We believe that <u>God</u> exists and is pleased with all who draw near by faith. We worship the one holy and loving God who is Father, Son, and Holy Spirit eternally." (4) (Article 1. God)

B. Proof texts: <u>I Peter 3:18</u>, <u>Luke 3:22</u>

7. Heaven And Hell

A. "We place our hope in the <u>reign of God</u> and its fulfillment in the day when Christ will come again in glory to judge the living and the dead...We await God's final victory...the resurrection of the dead, and a new heaven and a new earth...The righteous will rise to eternal life with God, and the unrighteous to hell and separation from God." (4) (Article 24. The Reign Of God)

B. Proof Texts: <u>Revelation 20:4-6</u>

THE MENNONITES SEEM TO HAVE A RIGHT DOCTRINE OF JESUS CHRIST, BUT HAVE A WORKS/COVENANT BASED SALVATION, WHICH IS NEVER SECURE. A FALSE WAY OF SALVATION MAKES THIS GROUP A FALSE DENOMINATION.

---

(1)   FAQ   About   Menonites,   https://www.mennoniteusa.org/who-are-mennonites/faq-about-mennonites/

(2) <u>Mennonite History</u>, http://www.anabaptists.org/history/mennohist.html

(3) <u>Amish</u>, https://en.wikipedia.org/wiki/Amish

(4) <u>Confession of Faith in a Mennonite Perspective</u>, 1995, 2014 http://mennoniteusa.org/confession-of-faith/

(5) BBC, Religions, Amish, https://www.bbc.co.uk/religion/religions/christianity/subdivisions/ amish_1.shtml#:~:text=Salvation%20came%20only%20by%20actual,community%20and%20through%20th e%20 ef%20in%20Jesus%20Christ.

(6) Eternal Security, http://thirdwaycafe.com/glossary/eternal-security/

(7)   Supportive   Communities   Network,   https://www.bmclgbt.org/ scn#:~:text=Supportive%20Communities%20Network%20%28SCN%29%20is%20a%20program%20of,affirmin

(8) Mennonite Church USA passes resolution committing to LGBTQ inclusion, https://religionnews.com/2022/06/02/mennonite-church-usa-passes-resolution-committing-to-lgbtq-inclusion/

DENOMINATIONS-Lesson 18

Methodist/United Methodist/Free Methodist/Wesleyan/Nazar-ene

Origin: "The United Methodist Church shares a common history and heritage with other Methodist and Wesleyan bodies. The lives and ministries of John Wesley and his brother, Charles, mark the origin of their common roots...Both...had transforming religious experiences in May, 1738." (1) (en/content/roots) "Though John Wesley originally wanted the Methodists to stay within the Church of England, the American Revolution decisively separated the Methodists in the American colonies from the life and sacraments of the English Church...Wesley sent...the Articles of Religion, which were received and adopted by the Baltimore Christmas Conference of 1784, officially establishing the Methodist Episcopal Church...On April 23, 1968, the United Methodist Church was created when the Evangelical United Brethren Church...and The Methodist Church...joined hands at the constituting General Conference in Dallas, Texas." (2) "The Church of the Nazarene traces its anniversary date to 1908..." (3) (Our Beginning) "The Free Methodist Church was birthed in 1860 when B. T. Roberts, a pastor in the Methodist Episcopal Church, could no longer serve in harmony with their practices...slaveholding, rent seats in the church, withhold women from full service in the church, and quench the movement of the Holy Spirit in public worship." (4) (Early Free Methodism)

Doctrinal Beliefs:

1. The Bible

A. "Article V. Holy Scripture containeth all things necessary to salvation" (1) (The Articles of Religion of the Methodist Church)

B. "The Bible is God's written Word, uniquely inspired by the Holy Spirit...it is the trustworthy record of God's revelation, and completely truthful...It has been faithfully preserved..." (4) (Authority)

C. Several translations of the Scriptures are quoted on Methodist websites mostly the NRSV[11], but also many others; NIV[1], NEB[2], and NASB[2].

D. Copyright for the New Revised Standard Version is held by the National Council of Churches, leaders in the ecumenical movement. This version deletes many complete verses; Acts 8:37(salvation), I John 5:7(trinity), Mark 15:28(fulfilled prophecy), Matthew 18:11(why Jesus came), and others.

E. Proof text: Deuteronomy 4:2

2. Salvation

A. "We are accounted righteous before God only for the merit of our Lord and Saviour Jesus Christ, by faith, and not for our own works...we are justified by faith, only..." (1) (The Articles of Religion of the Methodist Church)

B. "God, by His Spirit, acts to impart new life and put us into a relationship with himself as we repent..." (4) (New Life In Christ)

C. "Article XVI-The Sacraments...ordained of Christ...are certain signs of grace ...by which he doth work invisibly in us, and doth not only quicken, but also strengthen and confirm" (1) (The Articles of Religion of the Methodist Church)

D. "Water baptism and the Lord's Supper are the sacraments of the Church...They are means of grace through faith...By them, He works within us to quicken, strengthen, and confirm our faith." (4) (The Holy Sacraments)

E. "We believe that entire sanctification is that act of God, subsequent to regeneration, by which believers are made free from original sin, or depravity, and brought into a state of entire devotement to God, and the holy obedience of love made perfect." (3) (ARTICLES OF FAITH, CHRISTIAN HOLINESS AND ENTIRE SANCTIFICATION)

F. "After we have received the Holy Ghost, we may depart from grace given, and fall into sin..." (1) (The Articles of Religion of the Methodist Church) "The Christian can sin will-fully and sever his relationship with Christ." (4) (Restoration)

G. Proof Texts: Ephesians 2:8-9, John 5:24

3. Baptism

A. As seen in 2., C. & D. above, they believe that God uses baptism to "quicken" (make alive) the one being baptized.

B. "Methodist baptism is administered to both infants and adults, usually by sprinkling." (5) (Pg 39)

C. "Order for the Administration of Baptism to Infants: Dearly Beloved, forasmuch as God in his great mercy hath entered into covenant relation with man, wherein he hath included children as partakers of his gracious benefits...that he, being baptized with water, may also be baptized with the Holy Spirit, be received into Christ's holy Church..." (6) (The Psalter, The Ritual, Page 89)

D. Proof text: Acts 8:12

4. The Church

A. "We believe that the church is the body of Christ...'the communion of saints,' a community made up of all past, present, and future disciples of Christ."(1) (en/content/our-christian-roots-the-church)

B. "The church is created by God; it is the people of God." (4) (Church)

C. "The feminist movement exercises a powerful influence within the UMC. Women have been ordained to the ministry in...the UMC since 1956. As of 1992 they had 4,743 ordained women ministers...The new UMC worship book contains a number of references to God as both Mother and Father." (5) (Pg 52)

D. "Polls have shown that at least 30 percent of UMC ministers do not believe that Jesus Christ is God and 82% say they do not believe the Bible is the infallible Word of God....60% do not believe in the virgin birth...50% do not believe in the bodily resurrection of Christ...34% of Methodists believe community service is more important than proclaiming the Gospel." (5) (Pg 45)

E. "The Reconciling Ministries Network (RMN) is an organization seeking the inclusion of people of all sexual orientations and gender identities in both the policy and practices of United Methodist Church. The ministry has over 1100 affiliated congregations and 42,000 affiliated individuals. (2019)" (7)

F. Proof texts: <u>I Corinthians 14:33</u>, <u>I Timothy 3:1 & 4-5</u>, <u>Romans 1:26-27</u>

5. Jesus Christ

A. "Article II. The Son, who is the Word of the father, the very and eternal God ...took man's nature in the womb of the blessed Virgin...truly suffered, was crucified, dead, and buried to reconcile his Father to us." (1) (The Articles of Religion of the Methodist Church)

B. "Jesus of Nazareth was God in human flesh..." (4) (The Son-His Incarnation)

C. "United Methodist 'scholars' participated in the 'Jesus Seminar' which determined...Jesus did not believe that He was God...not born of a virgin, did not perform miracles, did not give prophecies of the future, did not die for man's sins, and did not rise from the dead." (5) (Pg 47)

D. Proof Texts: <u>John 1:14</u>, <u>I Corinthians 15:1-4</u>

6. The Trinity (Godhead)

A. "There is but one living and true God...three persons, of one substance, power, and eternity-the Father, the Son, and the Holy Ghost." (1) (The Articles of Religion of the Methodist Church) "There is but one living and true God...there are three persons: the Father, the Son, and the Holy Spirit." (4) (The Holy Trinity)

B. "In 1984 the UMC Women's Division issued an alternative Lord's Prayer: 'Our <u>Mother/Father</u>, who is everywhere, Holy be your names...'" (5) (Pg 53)

C. Proof texts: <u>John 17:1, 5, 11, 24, 25</u>

7. Heaven And Hell

A. "For those who <u>trust Him</u> and <u>obediently follow</u> Jesus as Saviour and Lord, there is a heaven of eternal glory and the blessedness of Christ's presence. But for the finally impenitent there is a hell of eternal suffering and of separation from God." (4) (Final Destiny)

B. Proof Text: <u>Luke 16:22-23</u>

THESE GROUPS SEEM TO HAVE A CORRECT STATED DOCTRINE OF JESUS CHRIST, BUT HAVE A SALVATION BASED ON FAITH, <u>PLUS</u> OBSERVING THE SACRAMENTS, <u>PLUS</u> ENTIRE SANCTIFICATION, <u>PLUS</u> TRYING TO KEEP THEM-SELVES SAVED BY NOT SINNING, WHICH MAKES THEM A FALSE DENOMINATION.

------

(1) <u>United Methodist Church Home Page</u>, http://www.umc.org

(2) <u>United Methodist Church-Wikipedia</u>, https://en.wikipedia.org/wiki/United_Methodist_Church

(3) <u>Church Of The Nazarene</u>, http://www.nazarene.org

(4) <u>We Believe</u>, https://fmcusa.org/webelieve

(5) <u>Protestant Denominations Today</u>, David W. Cloud, Way Of Life Literature, Port Huron, MI, 2014

(6) <u>The Methodist Hymnal</u>, The Methodist Book Concern, New York, Cincinnati, 1921

(7) <u>Reconciling Ministries Network</u>, https://en.wikipedia.org/wiki/Reconciling_Ministries_Network#:~:text=The%20Reconciling%20Ministries%20Network%20(RMN,American%20Christianity%20in%

DENOMINATIONS-Lesson 19

Muslim/Islam/Nation of Islam

Matthew 24:11

Origin: "Around the year 570 AD, Muhammad was born...In 610 God revealed His word to Muhammad through the Angel Gabriel. In this way, Muhammad became the chosen bearer of the divine message and began proclaiming the oneness of God. The name of this new religion, Islam, means "submission to God. The followers of Islam are called Muslims, meaning 'those who submit'." (1) (The Coming Of The Prophet) "...the first pillar of Islam is, 'There is no God but God (previously Allah) and Muhammad is the Messenger of God'." (1) (The Five Pillars Of Islam-Shahadah) "Islam is considered to be the fastest-growing religion in the world, and is rapidly becoming the second leading religion in the USA. 8 million Arab Muslims are now within the borders of the United States with over 1500 mosques; 800 new mosques...in the last 10 years. There are over 1.1 billion people in the world who are Muslim." (2) (pg 7) "The history of the Black Muslim Movement began with one Wallace Fard, an Islamic Negro, who in 1930 appeared among the Detroit Negro community." (3) (pg 262) "The main belief of The Nation of Islam and its followers is that there is only one god, whom they claim "came in the person" of Wallace Fard Muhammad[1]" (4) (Main Beliefs) "Muhammad died in 1975 and his son, Warith Deen Mohammed[2], became the leader of the Nation of Islam. (4) (Nation Of Islam) In 1978 Louis Farrakhan split from them to form his own Nation of Islam. "Farrakhan also claims to be Jesus Christ and Elijah, the prophet, in one person." (5) It was estimated in 2011 that the actual membership was 20,000-50,000.

Doctrinal Beliefs:

1. The Bible

---

1. https://en.wikipedia.org/wiki/Wallace_Fard_Muhammad

2. https://en.wikipedia.org/wiki/Warith_Deen_Mohammed

A. "1. The Torah which was revealed to Moses...2. The Gospel which Allah revealed to Jesus...3. The Psalms which Allah gave to David...4. Tablets of Abraham and Moses...5. The Glorious Qur'an which was revealed to His Prophet Muhammad, the Seal of the Prophets..." (6) (Books Known)

B. "The Qur'an is `confirming the scripture that was before it and stands as a guardian over it.' Thus, by the Qur'an, Allah abrogated all the previous Books. Allah has also guaranteed its protection from any play or mischievous distortion." (6) (The Qur'an Is Protected From Change)

C. "The previous scriptures were meant for a limited period that ended with the revelation of what abrogated them...they were not protected from corruption. They underwent distortion, addition and omission." (6) (Previous Scriptures Changed)

D. Proof texts: <u>Matthew 5:18</u>, <u>24:35</u>

2. Salvation

A. "The Prophet Muhammad said: Whoever believes there is no god but God (previously Allah), alone without partner, that Muhammad is His messenger, that Jesus is the servant and messenger of God, His word breathed into Mary and a spirit emanating from Him, and that Paradise and Hell are true, shall be received by God into Heaven." (1) (What Do Muslims Think About Jesus?)

B. "How Does Someone Become A Muslim? Simply by saying 'there is no god apart from God (Allah), and Muhammad is the Messenger of God.' By this declaration the believer announces his or her faith in all God's messengers, and the scriptures they brought. (1) (How Does Someone Become A Muslim)

C. Proof texts: <u>I John 4:1-3</u>, <u>Romans 10:9</u>

3. Baptism

A. "The word 'Baptism' comes from the Greek 'Baptein' which means 'to plunge, to immerse, or to wash.' It was an ancient custom to wash or to make ablution. Islam has preserved this tradition in the form of ablution and ritual *Ghusl* for the purpose of purification...*Yahya* (John, the Baptist) used to call people to repent and purify themselves in the River Jordan. It is mentioned that Je-sus also went to him and took a bath of purification (Mark 1:9-11)...For Jesus ...and his followers the Baptism was just a bath or ablution to purify themselves physically, ritually and spiritually..." (7)

B. Proof Text: <u>Matthew 28:19-20</u>

4. The Church

A. "The world's Muslims turn individually and collectively to Makkah, Islam's holiest city, to offer five daily prayers at dawn, noon, mid-afternoon, sunset and evening. In addition, Friday congregational service is also required. Although *salah* can be performed alone, it is meritorious to perform it with another or with a group. It is permissible to pray at home, at work, or even outdoors; however it is recommended that Muslims perform *salah* in a mosque." (1) (The Five Pillars Of Islam)

B. "There is no hierarchical authority in Islam, and no priests, so the prayers are led by a learned person who knows the Qur'an, chosen by the congregation." (1) (What Are The Five Pillars Of Islam-2. Prayer)

C. Proof texts: <u>Acts 2:41</u>, <u>Ephesians 5:25</u>

5. Jesus Christ

A. "There have been many prophets...Adam, Noah, Abraham, Lot, Ishmael, Isaac, Jacob, Joseph, Moses, Aaron, Elijah, Elias, David, Solomon, Jonah, Job, Zacharias, John, Jesus, and of course, the Last Messenger (Muhammad)." (6) (6. Messengers and Prophets)

B. "Muslims respect and revere Jesus...The Qur'an confirms his virgin birth... Truly, the likeness of Jesus with God is as the likeness of Adam..." (1) (What Do Muslims Think About Jesus?)

C. "...every Prophet is no more than a servant of God-they do not have a share in His Divinity." (6) (6. Messengers and Prophets)

D. "Islam rejects...the deity of Christ[3] and His Sonship, claiming that Jesus[4] was only a great prophet. Muhammad is considered to be the greatest prophet, whose coming was allegedly predicted by Christ." (John 16:7-11) (8) (Islam)

E. Proof texts: John 10:30-33, Romans 8:34

6. The Trinity (Godhead)

A. "Islam rejects the Trinity doctrine..." (8) (Islam)

B. "4. We believe in His Oneness...He has no associate in His Divinity, His Godship, His Names, or His Attributes." (6) (Our Creed)

C. "Of all His attributes, God emphasizes a single one above all others in His Final Book: that HE IS ONE. God is not two, three, four, or more beings. There is only one deity, and He is God." (6) (1. On The Nature of God)

D. Proof Texts: II Corinthians 13:14, John 14:16-17

7. Heaven And Hell

A. "Basic articles of faith include: the Day of Judgment, resurrection, Heaven and Hell." (1) (Understanding Islam-How Do Muslims View Death?)

B. "The Final Book contains many references on Paradise, and also on Hell, the destination of those people who knowingly reject God. Paradise is quite literally a place of indescribable joy, whereas Hell is its indescribable opposite... While the inhabitants of Paradise are permanent dwellers, the inmates of Hell are not necessarily imprisoned there forever; there are some who shall be ultimately freed...'There shall come out of Hell-fire he who has said, 'There is no deity except God' and has in his heart goodness weighing a barley-corn...a grain of wheat...an atom.'" (6) (4. The Presence of Evil)

B. Proof texts: Revelation 20:10 & 15

THIS RELIGION IS DEFINITELY A FALSE DENOMINATION WITH A WORKS-BASED SALVATION AND THE FALSE DOCTRINE THAT

---

3. http://www.wfial.org/index.cfm?fuseaction=archives.index&#Christ

4. http://www.wfial.org/index.cfm?fuseaction=archives.index&#Jesus

JESUS WAS ONLY A "MESSENGER OF ALLAH" AND LESS IMPORTANT THAN MUHAMMAD.

---

(1) Islam, https://saudiembassy.net/islam/#Islam%20And%20Muslims

(2) The Baptist Vision, publish monthly by The Temple Baptist Church, Powell, TN, June 1997 issue.

(3) The Kingdom of the Cults, Walter Martin, Bethany Fellowship, Minneapolis, MN, 1965, 1977.

(4) African-American Muslims, https://en.wikipedia.org/wiki/African-American_Muslims

(5) The Promise Keepers and Louis Farrakhan, The Last Trumpet Newsletter, David Meyer, June 1997.

(6) The Muslim's Official Creed of Islam, http://www.bible.ca/islam/islam-creed.htm

(7) How Does Islam View Baptism?, https://aboutislam.net/counseling/ask-the-scholar/muslim-creed/how-does-islam-view-baptism/

(8) Index of Cults and religions-Islam, http://www.watchman.org/index-of-cults-and-religions/#I

DENOMINATIONS-Lesson 20

Orthodox, Eastern (Greek, Russian, Antiochian)

M<u>ark 7:6-9</u>

Origin: In 1054 the "Eastern Church" (Orthodox) was officially separated from the "West-ern Church" (Roman Catholic) when "Pope Leo IX" issued a "sentence of anathema" against "Michael Cerularius, patriarch of Constantinople", for "evil doctrines and practices". (1) (pg 625-626) The main issues involved were unleavened bread, papal authority, Latin liturgies, and Roman additions to the Nicene Creed. All Orthodox branches together make up the world's second largest Christian denomination. "Orthodoxy believes that she has preserved and taught the historic Christian Faith, free from error and distortion, from the time of the Apostles." (2) There are about 6 million Orthodox in the United States.

Doctrinal Beliefs:

1. The Bible

A. "The Holy scriptures are highly regarded by the Orthodox Church...The Orthodox Church sees itself as the guardian and interpreter of the Scriptures... While the Bible is treasured as a valuable written record of God's revelation, it does not contain wholly that revelation...Scripture is part of the treasure of Faith which is known as Tradition...In addition to the...Scripture, the Orthodox Christian faith is celebrated in the Eucharist...expressed in prayers, hymns, and icons...embodied in the Nicene Creed..." (2) (Scriptures/Tradition)

B. "The most important creed in Christendom is the Nicene Creed...it contains the essence of New Testament teaching...The creeds give us a sure interpretation of the Scriptures against those who would distort them...the Nicene Creed constantly reminds the Orthodox Christian of what he personally believes, keeping his faith on track." (3) (Creed)

C. English translations used were the RSV, NKJV, NASB, Berkeley & TLB.

D. Proof text: <u>Mark 7:6-9</u>

2. Salvation

A. "Salvation begins with these three steps: 1) repent, 2) be baptized, and 3) receive the gift of the Holy Spirit...To be baptized means to be born again... The experience of salvation is initiated in the waters of baptism." (3) (Salvation/ Baptism)

B. "The Sacraments are seven in number. They are the visible means by which the invisible Grace of the Holy Spirit is imparted to us. Four Sacraments are <u>obligatory</u>: 1.Baptism, 2.Chrismation (anointment with holy oil), 3.Confession, and 4.Holy Communion. Three are <u>optional</u>: 1.Matrimony, 2.Holy Orders (Ordination) and 3.Unction (anointment of the sick)." (4) (The Sacraments)

C. "The Eucharist 'is the flesh of our Savior Jesus Christ, the flesh which suffered for our sins and which the Father in His graciousness raised from the dead.'" (5) (St. Ignatius of Antioch) "In the Eucharist, we partake mystically of Christ's Body and Blood, which impart His life and strength to us." (3) (Eucharist)

D. Proof text: <u>Acts 16:30-34</u>

3. Baptism

A. "I acknowledge one baptism for the forgiveness of sins." (2) (The Creed)

B. "BAPTISM...In it our sins are truly forgiven and we are energized by our union with Christ...The Orthodox Church practices baptism by full immersion." (3) (Baptism)

C. "The Sacrament of Baptism incorporates us into the Church, the Body of Christ...Through the three-fold immersion in the waters of Baptism in the Name of the Holy Trinity, one dies to the old ways of sin and is born to a new life in Christ...Following the custom of the early Church, Orthodoxy encourages the baptism of infants." (2) (Sacraments)

D. Proof Text: <u>Ephesians 2:8-9</u>

4. The Church

A. We believe "in one, holy, catholic and apostolic Church." (2) (The Creed)

B. "The True Church is composed of all who are in Christ—in heaven and on earth." (3) (Prayer To The Saints)

C. "There are fourteen Orthodox churches that are generally accepted as 'autocephalous,'...Greek...'self-headed'...the right to resolve all internal problems on its own authority and...to choose its own bishops, including the Patriarch, Archbishop or Metropolitan...these autocephalous Orthodox churches include the four ancient Eastern Patriarchates (Constantinople, Alexandria, Antioch, and Jerusalem), and ten other Orthodox churches...emerged over the centuries in Russia, Serbia, Romania, Bulgaria, Georgia, Cyprus, Greece, Poland, Albania, and the Czech and Slovak Republics." (6) (I. Introduction)

D. "Mary is called *Theotokos, meaning* 'God-bearer' or 'Mother of God'...we honor her highly as the model of holiness, the first of the redeemed..." (3) (Mary)

E. "Prayer to the saints is encouraged...we pray to the saints who have departed this life, seeking their prayers." (3) (Prayer To The Saints)

F. "...transubstantiation. The consecrated bread is declared to be the identical body as it walked among men and was crucified and the consecrated wine to be the identical blood that was shed on the cross." (1) (pg 630)

G. Proof texts: <u>Acts 2:41</u>, <u>Ephesians 5:25</u>

5. Jesus Christ

A. "Jesus Christ is the Second Person of the Holy Trinity...Who for us men and for our salvation came down from heaven, and was incarnate of the Holy Spirit and the Virgin Mary...was crucified...suffered...and was buried...the third day

He rose again... ascended into heaven...sits at the right hand of the Father...He shall come again..." (3) (Jesus Christ)

B. "Baptism is the way in which a person is actually united to Christ." (3) (Baptism)

C. "We believe that Our Lord Jesus Christ is truly God. He is Jesus, that is, the Savior and Christ, the Lord's Anointed, a Son not created of another substance, as is the case with us, but a Son begotten of the very substance of the Father before all time..." (7)

D. Proof Text: I Corinthians 15:1-4

6. The Trinity (Godhead)

A. "GOD THE FATHER is the fountainhead of the Holy Trinity. The Scriptures reveal the one God is Three Persons—Father, Son, and Holy Spirit—eternally sharing the one divine nature. From the Father the Son is begotten before all ages and all time. It is from the Father that the Holy Spirit eternally proceeds." (3) (God the Father)

B. "We believe that God is One in substance and Triune in persons. We worship One God in Trinity...God the Father is the prime cause of creation and God the Son and God the Holy Spirit took part in creation..." (7)

C. Proof Texts: II Corinthians 13:14, I John 5:7

7. Heaven And Hell

A. "At death man's body goes to the earth from which it was taken, and the soul, being conscious and exercising all its faculties immediately after death, are judged by God. This judgment following man's death we call the Particular Judgment. The final reward of men, however, we believe will take place at the time of the General Judgment. During the time between the Particular and the General Judgment, which is called the Intermediate State, the souls of men have foretaste of their blessing or punishment." (7)

B. "Heaven is the place of God's throne...the abode of God's angels as well as of the saints who have passed from this life...The Orthodox Church under-stands hell as a place of eternal torment for those who willfully reject the grace of God." (3) (Heaven/Hell)

C. Proof text: Luke 16:22-23

THIS DENOMINATION IS A FALSE DENOMINATION THAT TEACHES SALVATION THROUGH KEEPING THE SACAMENTS, SPECIFICALLY "BAPTISM" AND "THE HOLY EUCHARIST". ALSO, TRADITION IS AS VALUABLE TO THEM AS THE SCRIPTURES!

---

(1) A Manual of Church History, Volume I, Albert Henry Newman, Judson Press, Valley Forge, 1902, 1931, 1972.

(2) Teachings of the Orthodox Church, https://www.goarch.org/-/teachings-of-the-orthodox-church

(3) Orthodox Creed, http://www.bible.ca/cr-Orthodox#creed

(4) Introduction: What Is The Greek Orthodox Church?, https://www.goarch.org/-/introduction-what-is-the-greek-orthodox-church-

(5) The Church Fathers on the Holy Eucharist, http://ww1.antiochian.org/church-fathers-holy-eucharist

(6) Organization and Hierarchy of Autocephalous Orthodox Churches, centered at Constantinople, http://www.bible.ca/orthodox-church-autocephalous-hierarchy-organization.htm

(7) An Outline Of The Orthodox Faith, https://www.goarch.org/-/an-outline-of-the-orthodox-faith?inheritRedirect=true

DENOMINATIONS-Lesson 21

Pentecostal

(Church of God in Christ [1897-6,800], Pentecostal Holiness [1898-8383], Church of God of Prophecy [1907-10,000], Assemblies of God [1914-248,000], Foursquare Gospel [1923-25,577], Full Gospel [1951-part of Assemblies of God], Vineyard Chur-ches [1983-2500])

<u>Matthew 7:21-23</u>

The numbers above in [ ] are the year organized and the number of churches worldwide.

Origin: "When the Southern Methodist Church rejected the holiness movement in 1894, over 25 new holiness groups were formed in the United States...The modern pentecostal movement had its origins in Topeka, Kansas, in a small Bible school conducted by Charles Fox Parham, a holiness evangelist who began his ministry as a Methodist pastor. In 1901, Agnes Ozman, a student at Parham's school, received the baptism in the Holy Spirit accompanied by speaking in tongues...The pentecostal movement received world-wide influence in 1906 in Los Angeles, California, in the Azuza Street Revival led by the African-American holiness evangelist William Joseph Seymour. From Azuza Street, the pentecostal experience spread around the world..." (1) The doctrinal statements of these groups contain no major doctrinal differences.

Doctrinal Beliefs:

1. The Bible

A. "Article Five. We believe in the verbal and plenary inspiration of the Holy Scriptures..." (2)

B. "The Bible is the inspired Word of God, a revelation from God to man, the infallible rule of faith and conduct..." (3) (Article VII. Statement Of Fundamental Truths, 1. The Scriptures Inspired)

C. "1. The Scriptures Inspired. The Scriptures, both the Old and New Testaments, are verbally inspired of God and are the revelation of God to man, the infallible, authoritative rule of faith and conduct." (4)

D. Most Pentecostal Churches today use the modern English Bible Translations.

E. Proof text: <u>2 Timothy 3:16-17</u>

2. Salvation

A. "Article Eight. We believe, teach and firmly maintain the scriptural doctrine of justification by faith alone" (2)

B. "We believe that the Baptism of the Holy Ghost is an experience subsequent to conversion...We believe that we are not baptized with the Holy Ghost in order to be saved...we believe...that a Holy Ghost experience is mandatory for all men today. (5) (The Baptism Of The Holy Ghost)

C. "Therefore, on the basis of Scriptural precedent, and guided by our original Foursquare teaching, we affirm that the initial physical evidence of the Baptism in the Holy Spirit is that of speaking in other tongues." (6)

D. "9. Sanctification. Sanctification is an act of separation from that which is evil, and of dedication unto God...The Scriptures teach a life of 'holiness without which no man shall see the Lord'....By the power of the Holy Ghost we are able to obey the command: 'Be ye holy, for I am holy.'" (4)

E. This belief in sinless perfection after being born again <u>to keep your salvation</u> is almost universal in Pentecostal denominations. Other statements on this subject: "...salvation from sin and sinning." (2) (Article Seven), "...heaven is a portion of the reward of the finally righteous..." (2) (Article Six), "...man is saved by confession and forsaking his sins..." (5) (man)

F. "The General Council of the Assemblies of God disapproves of the unconditional security position which holds that it is impossible for a person once save to be lost...2. Salvation is received <u>and kept</u> by faith...4. The believer's salvation is forfeited by rejecting Christ." (7) (Pg 107-108)

G. Proof texts: <u>Acts 10:43-48</u>, <u>1 Corinthians 13:8</u>, <u>1 John 1:8-10</u>

3. Baptism

A. "6. Ordinances of the Church. The ordinance of baptism by immersion is commanded in the Scriptures. All who repent and believe on Christ as Savior and Lord are to be baptized." (4)

B. "As Pentecostals, we practice immersion in preference to 'SPRINKLING', because immersion corresponds more closely to the Death, Burial, and Resurrection of our Lord..." (5) (Ordinances of the Church, C. Water Baptism)

C. Proof Text: <u>Acts 8:35-38</u>

4. The Church

A. "We believe in one, holy, universal Church. All who repent of their sins and confess Jesus as Lord and Savior are regenerated by the Holy Spirit and form the living Body of Christ, of which he is the head and of which we are all members." (8) (The Church: The Instrument of the Kingdom)

B. "From its inception the 'latter rain' Pentecostal movement has been characterized by doctrinal heresy, exaggeration, and deception...Those who claim that the apostolic Pentecostal signs have been restored are forced to accept the occultic/hypnotic phenomenon such as spirit slaying and drunkenness and soothsaying (which they often call 'the word of knowledge') as apostolic signs...This is exactly what we see occurring in the latest manifestation of the latter rain movement, the Laughing Revival." (9)

C. The Foursquare Church was established in 1923 by a woman named Aimee Semple McPherson. "In The Foursquare Church in the U.S., 37 percent of all credentialed ministers are female" (10)

D. Proof Texts: <u>Galatians 1:1-2</u>, <u>1 Corinthians 14:29-35</u>

5. Jesus Christ

A. "We believe in one Lord, Jesus Christ, the only Son of God, eternally begotten of the Father. All things were made through Him and for Him. He is true God and true man. He...was born of the virgin, Mary. He suffered, died, was buried, and on the third day He rose from the dead. He ascended to the right hand of the Father, and He will return to judge the living and the dead." (11)

6. The Trinity (Godhead)

A. "Christ taught a distinction of Persons in the Godhead which He expressed in specific terms of relationship, as Father, Son, and Holy Ghost..." (3) (Article VII. Statement Of Fundamental Truths, 2. The One True God, (b). Distinction and Relationship in the Godhead)

B. "WE BELIEVE in the Holy Trinity—one God, eternally existing in Three Persons: Father, Son, and Holy Spirit." (11)

C. Proof Texts: <u>Luke 3:22</u>

7. Heaven And Hell

A. "After Christ returns to reign, He will bring about the final defeat of Satan and all of his minions and works, the resurrection of the dead, the final judgment and the eternal blessing of the righteous and eternal conscious punishment of the wicked." (8) (The Kingdom of God and the Final Judgment)

B. "Article Six. We believe that eternal life with God in heaven is a portion of the reward of the finally righteous; and that everlasting banishment from the presence of the Lord and unending torture in hell are the wages of the persistently wicked." (2)

C. Proof text: <u>2 Thessalonians 1:7-10</u>

THESE GROUPS HAVE A CORRECT DOCTRINE OF JESUS CHRIST, BUT THEY TEACH THE ERRORS OF NO ETERNAL

SECURITY AND A MANDATORY "BAPTISM OF THE HOLY GHOST" EVIDENCED BY SPEAKING IN TONGUES AFTER SALVAT-ION. ADDING CONDITIONS NECESSARY TO SALVATION MAKES THEM A FALSE DENOMINATION.

---

(1) <u>IPHC Spiritual Heritage</u>, https://alphaiphc.org/iphc-spiritual-heritage/

(2) <u>IPHC Articles of Faith</u>, https://iphc.org/beliefs/ (International Pentecostal Holiness Church)

(3) Full Gospel Assemblies[1], <u>Constitution and Bylaws</u>, https://fgai.org/about/constitution-and-bylaws/

(4) <u>Official Creed of the Assemblies of God</u>, http://www.bible.ca/cr-assemblies-of-god

(5) <u>What We Believe</u>, https://www.cogic.org/about-us/what-we-believe/ (Church Of God In Christ)

(6) <u>Spirit Baptism – A Clarification, International Church of the Four-Square Gospel</u>, http://withchrist.org/Spirit%20Baptism.htm

(7) <u>Where We Stand, Assemblies Of God</u>, Published by Gospel Publishing House, Springfield, Missouri, August 1, 2003.

(8) <u>Vineyard-Core Values And Beliefs, Our Statement Of Faith</u>, https://vineyardusa.org/ about/ core-values-beliefs/

(9) <u>The Strange History of Pentecostalism, Part 1 of 3</u>, August 3, 1998 (David W. Cloud, Fundamental Baptist Information Service, P.O. Box 610368, Port Huron, MI.

(10) <u>More Female Senior Pastors Than Ever Before, Study Finds</u>, https://resources. foursquare.org/ more_female_senior_pastors_than_ever_before_study_finds/

(11) <u>Church Of God Of Prophecy-Doctrine</u>, http://cogop.org/about/doctrine/

---

1. https://fgai.org/

DENOMINATIONS-Lesson 22

Plymouth Brethren

Matthew 18:20

Origin: "The Plymouth Brethren is a Christian movement which originated in England in the 19th century...can be traced to 1827 when John Nelson Darby (1800-1882) and three other men began to conduct Bible studies and to break bread together in Dublin...He left the Anglican Church..." (1) Then in 1832 B.W. Newton, the leader of one of the larger assemblies located in Plymouth, England, invited Darby to come and share the ministry. This he did...From 1832 to 1845 Darby was in fellowship with and ministered occasionally to the thriving Ebrington Street assembly...It was considered the center of the Brethren movement and grew to number 1,200 communicants...During this first twenty years these groups, known as assemblies, were established worldwide. In their New Testament simplicity they preferred to designate themselves 'brethren', but the influence of the Plymouth center soon caused them to be known as the, 'Plymouth Brethren.'" (2)

"As a result of a division in England in 1848 there are two basic types of Brethren assemblies, commonly known as exclusive and open. Led in the beginning by Darby, the exclusive assemblies produced most of the movements well-known Bible teachers...Open assemblies were led by George Muller, well known for his orphanages and life of faith...Today there are an estimated 850 open assemblies in the U.S. with only 250 exclusive." (1) "The Open Brethren...maintain the same doctrinal foundations and Body of truth as the exclusives, with the exception of the one doctrine that divides them. The opens consider each of their assemblies to be independent of the others as to its government and actions..." (2)

Doctrinal Beliefs:

1. The Bible

A. "In no uncertain terms the Brethren proclaimed the Scriptures to be absolutely inspired by God and the sole authority for faith and practice." (2)

B. "A number of doctrines and positions generally characterize the 'Brethren'... verbal, plenary inspiration of the original manuscripts of the Bible." (3)

C. The Darby English Translation was published in 1890. It was one of the earliest translations after Wescott and Hort completed their textually critical text. Darby was influenced by their work, deleting I John 5:7 and Acts 2:37 completely. The KJV has hell 54 times in the entire Bible, but the Darby Translation has hell only 12 times. Hell is replaced by "sheol" 31 times in the Old Testament. Hell is changed to "hades" 10 times, and "pit of gloom" 1 time in the New Testament. Also, C. I. Scofield, editor of the Scofield Reference Bible, was a Plymouth Brethren and his study notes were influenced by their beliefs.

D. Proof text: <u>II Timothy 3:16</u>, <u>Revelation 22:19</u>

2. Salvation

A. "It was mainly through Darby's ministry and writings that the sovereignty of God, election, assurance, acceptance, and unconditional eternal security were built into the movement...Darby strongly emphasized the indwelling of the Holy Spirit at the time of the new birth..." (2)

B. "Most open assemblies hold a middle of the road position with respect to election and free-will. Some can be found at either extreme. Most exclusive meetings hold to election...Most hold to the doctrine of Eternal Security." (3)

C. Proof texts: <u>I Timothy 2:3-6</u>, <u>I John 2:1-2</u>

3. Baptism

A. "...there is one doctrine and practice which is held by all Open Brethren assemblies—except perhaps by one or two of exclusive origin—which is that baptism must be only for believers of a responsible age on confession of faith ...if he was baptized as an infant it does not count in their eyes. The doctrine of household baptism is rigidly rejected and no teaching of it would be allowed.

Some meetings might tolerate an individual who held such a view, but he would have to keep quiet on the subject." (4)

B. "A number of doctrines and positions generally characterize the 'Brethren'... believers baptism by immersion. A significant number of brethren in the 'non-open' assemblies believe in and practice household baptism." (3) [Household baptism is the teaching that in Acts 16:15, 16:32-33 and 18:8 some small children and infants must have been baptized with their households, thereby justifying infant baptism.]

C. "Darby strongly emphasized...the truth that believers are baptized into the one Body, the Church." (2)

D. Proof Texts: <u>Acts 8:12</u>, <u>18:8</u>

4. The Church

A. "Eventually, Darby's followers created a tight group of churches known as Exclusive Brethren (also called Darbyites), while the others, maintaining a more congregational church government with less stringent membership standards, were called Open Brethren." (5) (Page 3)

B. "Open Brethren churches are 'completely' independent without any form of higher governing body. Each church observes the ecclesiastical offices of Elder and Deacon, but not salaried ministry. 'Gifted Brothers' officiate worship and communion services, and 'Gifted Sisters' lead private Bible studies." (6)

C. "Exclusive or Closed Brethren shun the idea of independence and maintain circles of fellowship without a higher governing body. They do not have Elders, but instead utilize the talents of 'leading brothers.'" (6)

D. Some of the distinctives of the Plymouth Brethren movement are as follows: 1. The remembrance meeting held each Sunday, during which the Lord's Supper is received...2. Though the Brethren believe in preachers, they do not believe in strong pastoral leadership. The assemblies are ruled by a plurality of elders. (1)

E. "Then there is the plight of the 'sistern', the Brethren women. The assemblies have always insisted upon female silence in the meetings and submission in the home...The Brethren still insist that their women wear head coverings as a sign of submission...a bit of net or cloth doily..." (2)

F. Proof Texts: Revelation 1:10-11, Philippians 1:1

5. Jesus Christ

A. "You cannot address Jesus directly as the eternal Son of God without also accepting His Virgin Birth, sinless life, atoning sacrifice, triumphant resurrection and imminent Second Advent." (7) (Volume 7 by W. Morrison)

B. Proof Text: I Timothy 3:16

6. The Trinity (Godhead)

A. "First of all these brethren hold tenaciously to the historic fundamental doctrines of Christianity, the Holy Trinity, Father, Son and Holy Spirit, co-equal and co-eternal, the essential deity and true impeccable humanity of the Lord Jesus Christ" (7) (Volume 6 by T.E. Wilson)

B. Proof Texts: Acts 10:38, I Peter 1:2

7. Heaven And Hell

A. "They believe in heaven for the regenerate and eternal punishment for the Christ-rejector" (7) (Volume 6 by T.E. Wilson)

B. "They believe...in a heaven for the saved, and a hell for the unrepentant who die in their sins. (7) (Volume 4 by Harold Mackay)

C. Proof text: I Thessalonians 4:16-18

THE PLYMOUTH BRETHREN ARE A FALSE RELIGION SINCE MANY ARE IN ERROR ABOUT ELECTION (SALVATION PREDETERMINED-NO CHOICE), BAPTISM AND THE CHURCH.

____

(1) Denominations Today, Brethren (2) Plymouth Brethren, https://www.wayoflife.org/database/denominations_today.html

(2) The Plymouth Brethren-A Brief History, Miles J. Stanford, http://www.biblebeliever .co.za/Brethren%20History/The%20Plymouth%20Brethren%20%20A%20Brief%20History.htm

(3) What is the doctrinal position of the (Plymouth)"Brethren"?, https://brethrenonline.org/home/articles/plymouth-brethren-faq/

(4) The "Brethren" since 1870, The Open Brethren, http://biblecentre.org/content.php?mode=7&item=908

(5) Christianity Today, Christian History, John Nelson Darby, https://docslib.org/doc/ 407659/john-nelson-darby-father-of-dispensationalism

(6) Brethren Groups, Plymouth Brethren-1825, http://www.cob-net.org/docs/groups.htm

(7) Who are the brethren?, http://www.believershome.com/christian-resources.php

DENOMINATIONS-Lesson 23

Presbyterian

———

Presbyterian Church U.S.A.[1983-10,000], Presbyterian Church in America[1973-1345], Associate Reformed Presbyterian Church[1782-250], Free Presbyterian Church[1951-100], Cumberland Presbyterian Church[1810-982]

Romans 10:12-13

The numbers in [ ] above indicate the year of organization and the number of churches.

Origin: "John Knox, a Scotsman who studied with Calvin in Geneva, Switzerland, took Calvin's teachings back to Scotland...The Presbyterian church traces its ancestry back primarily to Scotland and England." (1) (What We Believe/Church History) The Presbyterian Church U.S.A., after referred to as PC-USA, is by far the largest, most liberal, and most ecumenical of the Presbyterian churches. They alone are members of the National Council of Churches and the World Council of Churches. They are the only ones who ordain women as deacons, elders and ministers. We will focus on the PC(USA) as they make up over 80% of Presbyterians and share basic doctrines with most of them. All the listed churches hold to a "reformed theology" based on the <u>Westminster Confession Of Faith</u> [1647] except for the Cumberland Presbyterian Church which modified it in 1814 "...to eliminate...the doctrine of universal foreordination...unconditional election and reprobation, limited atonement...the features of hyper-Calvinism..." (2)

Doctrinal Beliefs:

1. The Bible

A. "Chapter I, Sec. VIII. The Old Testament in Hebrew...and the New Testament in Greek...inspired by God and by His singular care and providence kept pure in all ages, are therefore authentical..." (3)

B. "...the Free Presbyterian Church has, throughout its history, used the Authorized (often called the "King James") Version of the Scriptures." (4-Free Presbyterian Church) (Pg 63)

C. "The KJV was written in the everyday language of its time...revised in the late 19th century...numerous...translations into English have been published since then. Many PCUSA congregations use the Revised Standard Version (RSV) or the New Revised Standard Version (NRSV), though PCUSA congregations are permitted to use other translations, as determined by the congregation." (1) (What We Believe/ Theology/Bible/Translations)

D. Proof text: Psalms 12:6-7

2. Salvation

A. "Chapter III, Sec. III. By the decree of God, for the manifestation of His glory, some men and angels are predestinated unto everlasting life, and others fore-ordained to everlasting death." (3)

B. "Chapter VII, Sec. III. He freely offereth unto sinners life and salvation by Jesus Christ; requiring of them faith in Him, that they may be saved, and promising to give unto all those that are ordained unto eternal life His Holy Spirit, to make them willing, and able to believe." (3)

C. "Chapter X, Sec. I. All those whom God hath predestined unto life, and those only, He is pleased in His appointed and accepted time effectually to call...to grace and salvation by Jesus Christ..." (3)

D. "Chapter X, Sec. IV. Others, not elected, although they may be called by the ministry of the Word, and may have some common operations of the Spirit, yet they never truly come unto Christ, and therefore cannot be saved..." (3)

E. "The Westminster Confession reflected John Calvin's system of predestinarian theology...summarized in five points by the acronym of TULIP: Total depravity of man, meaning man is incapable of responding to the Gospel; Unconditional election, meaning God chooses which men will be saved and which men will be lost; Limited atonement, meaning Christ died only for those who will be saved; Irresistible grace, meaning the sinner cannot resist God's call to salvation; and Perseverance of the saints, meaning those who are saved will hold out faithful to the end. (4-Presbyterian) (Pg 58-59)

F. Proof texts: <u>I Timothy 2:3-6</u>

3. Baptism

A. "Chapter XXVIII, Sec. I. Baptism is a sacrament of the New Testament, ordained by Jesus Christ, not only for the solemn admission of the party baptized into the visible Church; but also, to be unto him a <u>sign and seal</u> of the <u>covenant of grace</u>..."..."Chapter XXVIII, Sec. III. Dipping of the person into the water is not necessary; but Baptism is rightly administered by pouring or sprinkling water upon the person." (3)

B. "baptism should be administered to believers and to their children...are included in God's covenant with His people" (4-Baptism) (Pg 64)

C. "On the mode of baptism...The Free Presbyterian Church...hereby affirms that each member...shall have liberty to decide for himself which course to adopt on these controverted issues..." (4) (Pg 64)

D. Proof Texts: <u>Mark 1:9-11</u>

4. The Church

A. "Chapter XXV, Sec. 1. The catholic or universal Church which is <u>invisible</u>, consists of the whole number of the elect that have been, are, or shall be gathered into one, under Christ the Head thereof..." (3)

B. "Chapter XXV, Sec. 2. The <u>visible</u> Church, which is also catholic or universal under the Gospel...consists of all those throughout the world that profess the true religion; and of their children..." (3)

C. "...Calvin developed the *presbyterian* pattern of church government, which vests governing authority primarily in elected lay persons known as elders. The word *presbyterian* comes from the Greek word for elder...Elders are chosen by the people. The body of elders elected to govern a particular congregation is called a *session*...Presbyterian elders are both elected and ordained... other governing bodies are presbyteries, which are composed of several churches; synods, which are composed of several presbyteries; and the General Assembly, which represents the entire denomination." (1) (What we Believe) (What makes us unique?) (Church Government)

D. "a formal policy that allows for homosexuals to be received as members, and even allows for the ordination of homosexuals as long as they do not engage in same-sex relationships." (4-The PC_USA and Homosexuality) (Pg 68)

E. "Presbyterians participated in the production of the National Council of Churches inclusive language lectionary, which removed masculine references to God; addressed God as 'Father and Mother'; deleted passages which instruct the wife to submit to the husband...and they question whether the worship of a redeemer who is male is possible or healthy for women...PC-USA was a chief sponsor of the World Council of Churches 'Re-imaging conference'...A key theme was the celebration of Sophia, the supposed goddess of creation. The conferees joined together in repeating a prayer to Sophia, including the words: 'Our maker Sophia.'" (4-The PC-USA and Paganism) (Pg 72)

F. Proof Texts: <u>Romans 1:26-27 & 32, 16:3-5</u>

5. Jesus Christ

A. "Chapter VIII, Sec. II & IV. The Son of God, the second person in the Trinity, being very and eternal God...conceived by the power of the Holy Ghost...of the virgin Mary...He was made under the law and did perfectly fulfill it...was crucified, and died; was buried...On the third day He rose from the dead...ascended into heaven...making intercession." (3)

B. Proof Text: <u>Galatians 4:4-5</u>

6. The Trinity (Godhead)

A. "Chapter II, Sec. III. In the unity of the Godhead there be three persons...God the Father, God the Son, and God the Holy Ghost." (3)

B. Proof Texts: <u>I Peter 1:2</u>

7. Heaven And Hell

A. "Chapter XXXIII, Sec. II. For then shall the righteous go into everlasting life... but the wicked who know not God, and obey not the Gospel of Jesus Christ, shall be cast into eternal torments." (3)

B. Proof text: <u>John 5:24-25, 28-29</u>

THESE GROUPS HAVE A CORRECT DOCTRINE OF JESUS CHRIST, BUT MOST TEACH SALVATION BY ELECTION, HOLDING TO THE DOCTRINES OF A UNIVERSAL CHURCH AND INFANT BAPTISM, MAKING THEM FALSE DENOMINATIONS.

---

(1) <u>Presbyterian Church (U.S.A)</u>, https://www.presbyterianmission.org/

(2) <u>Confession of Faith Cumberland Presbyterian Churches</u>, Preface to1883,

http://www.cumberland.org/gao/confession/confess.htm#1984%20Confession [1]

(3) <u>Westminster Confession of Faith</u>, http://www.freepres.org/westminster.htm

(4) <u>Protestant Denominations Today</u>, Presbyterian, David W. Cloud, Fundamental Baptist News Service, Oak Harbor, WA, 1996, https://www.wayoflife.org/free_ebooks/protestant_denominations_today.php

---

1. http://www.cumberland.org/gao/confession/

confess.htm#a5c02393e59c943d6a75a9241140faca31984_0bcef9c45bd8a48eda1b26eb0c61c869_20Confession

DENOMINATIONS-Lesson 24

Reformed

―――

I **I Peter 3:9**

Reformed Church In America [300,000], Protestant Reformed Churches In America [6,000], Christian Reformed Church [268,000], Free Reformed Churches Of North America [3,400] (Numbers in [ ] indicate membership.) (All groups listed above share the same roots and basic beliefs.)

Origin: "The Reformed branch of Protestantism is rooted in the Reformation of the 1500s. Its primary leader was John Calvin of Switzerland, whose reform movement spread to Scotland, where it became the Presbyterian Church, and the Netherlands, where it became the Dutch Reformed Church...in the small colonial town of New Amsterdam (New York), on a Sunday in 1628, about fifty people gathered...marks the birthdate of the Reformed Church in America." (1) "The oldest of the doctrinal standards of the Christian Reformed Church is the Confession Of Faith, popularly known as the Belgic Confession...The confession's chief author was Guido de Bres, a preacher of the Reformed churches of the Nether-lands...in the year 1561...The text, not the contents, was revised...at the Synod Of Dort in 1618-19 and adopted as one of the doctrinal standards to which all officebearers in the Reformed churches were required to subscribe." (2) (Introduction) (The Belgic Confession condemns "Anabaptists" three times.) "we willingly accept the three ecumenical creeds-the Apostles', Nicene, and Athanasian." (2) (Article 9)

"The Reformed Church in America has over 300,000 members and is a founding member of the National Council of Churches and the World Council of Churches. " (3)

Doctrinal Beliefs:

1. The Bible

A. "We confess that this Word of God was not sent nor delivered by the will of men, but that holy men of God spoke, being moved by the Holy

Spirit...Afterwards our God—because of the special care he has for us and our salvation -commanded his servants, the prophets and apostles, to commit this revealed Word to writing. He himself wrote with his own finger the two tables of the law. Therefore we call such writings holy and divine Scriptures." (2) (Article 3)

B. "Over the years, synods of the CRCNA have approved a number of Bible translations for use in worship by Christian Reformed congregations...King James Version (KJV)...American Standard Version (ASV)...Revised Standard Version (RSV)...New International Version (NIV)...New Revised Standard Version (NRSV)...Today's New International Version (TNIV)...English Standard Version (ESV)...New Living Translation (NLT)" (4)

C. The KJV has "hell" 54 times, but these other translations have "hell" only 13-14 times!!! Usually it was changed to "sheol" (OT) or "hades" (NT).

D. Proof Texts: <u>II Peter 1:20-21</u>, <u>Revelation 22:19</u>

2. Salvation

A. "We believe that by the disobedience of Adam original sin has been spread through the whole human race...an inherited depravity..." (2-Article 15)

B. "We believe that—all Adam's descendants having thus fallen...God...is merciful...<u>saving</u> from this perdition those whom he, in his eternal and unchangeable counsel, has <u>elected</u> and <u>chosen</u>...without any consideration of their works. He is just in leaving the others in their ruin and fall into which they plunged themselves." (2) (Article 16)

C. "The Synod of Dort (1618)...summarized Calvinist doctrine in five points: 1) Total Depravity of Man, 2) Unconditional Election, 3) Limited Atonement, 4) Irresistible Grace, 5) Perseverance of the Saints. These five points are often referred to by the acronym "TULIP."" (3)

D. "We believe...God...has ordained sacraments for us to seal his promises in us...to nourish and sustain our faith...For they are visible signs and seals...by... which God works in us through the power of the Holy Spirit." (2) (Article 33)

E. Proof Texts: <u>Romans 10:12-13</u>, <u>I Timothy 2:3-6</u>, <u>I John 2:1-2</u>, <u>Titus 3:5</u>

3. Baptism

A. "Having abolished circumcision...he established in its place the sacrament of baptism. By it we are received into God's church." (2) (Article 34)

B. "the RCA affirms sprinkling, immersion, and pouring as methods of baptism... The RCA baptizes infants as well as older children and adults. Baptism is primarily an act of God, showing grace toward us..." (5)

C. "...we believe that anyone who aspires to reach eternal life ought to be baptized only once without ever repeating it...For that reason we detest the error of the Anabaptists who are not content with a single baptism once received and also condemn the baptism of the children of believers" (2) (Article 34)

D. Proof Texts: <u>Acts 8:12, 36-38</u> (Verse 37 is missing from the RSV, NIV, NRSV, NLT, ESV and the TNIV, which are approved translations.)

4. The Church

A. "We believe and confess one single catholic or universal church...not confined , bound, or limited to a certain place or certain persons. But it is spread and dispersed throughout the entire world..." (2) (Article 27)

B. "There should be ministers or pastors to preach the Word of God and administer the sacraments. There should also be elders and deacons, along with the pastors, to make up the council of the church." (2) (Article 30)

C. "Women have...a vital role in the RCA...Today they are missionaries, teachers, study leaders, volunteers, elders, deacons, and pastors...Nearly 50 percent of the students in RCA seminaries are women (1)

D. Proof Texts: <u>Acts 9:31</u>, <u>I Corinthians 16:19</u>, <u>Philippians 1:1</u>

5. Jesus Christ

A. "We believe that Jesus Christ, according to his divine nature, is the only Son of God-eternally begotten, not made or created...and Jesus Christ already existed before creating all things." (2) (Article 10)

B. "And Christ not only assumed human nature as far as the body is concerned but also a real human soul...Therefore we confess, against the heresy of the Anabaptists who deny that Christ assumed human flesh from his mother" (2) (Article 18) (Baptists have always believed that Jesus was perfect God in the flesh, not having a human soul, but a divine soul.)

C. "We believe that Jesus Christ...offering himself on the tree of the cross and pouring out his precious blood for the cleansing of our sins..." (2) (Article 21)

D. "We believe that we have no access to God except through the one and only Mediator and Intercessor: Jesus Christ the Righteous." (2) (Article 26)

E. Proof Texts: <u>Philippians 2:5-8</u>, <u>I John 4:2</u>

6. The Trinity (Godhead)

A. "...we believe in one God, who is one single essence, in who there are three persons, really, truly, and eternally distinct according to their incommunicable properties—namely, Father, Son, and Holy Spirit." (2) (Article 8)

B. Proof Texts: <u>II Corinthians 13:14</u>, <u>I John 5:7</u> (missing in the RSV, NIV, NRSV, NLT, ESV and TNIV, which are approved translations)

7. Heaven And Hell

A. "Finally we believe, according to God's Word, that when the time appointed by the Lord is come...and the number of the elect is complete, Christ will come from heaven, bodily and visibly, as he ascended, with great glory and majesty, to declare himself the judge of the living and the dead...Then all hu-man creatures will appear in person before the great judge...who have lived from the beginning to the end of the world." (2) (Article 37) (General Judgment)

B. "The evil ones...shall be made immortal-but only to be tormented in the everlasting fire prepared for the devil and his angels." (2) (Article 37)

C. "In contrast, the faithful and elect will be crowned with glory and honor. The Son of God will 'confess their names' before God his Father and the holy and elect angels…And as a gracious reward the Lord will make them possess a glory such as the heart of man could never imagine." (2) (Article 37)

D. Proof Texts: <u>II Timothy 4:1</u>, <u>Revelation 20:4-6, 11-12</u>

THESE GROUPS HAVE AN INCORRECT DOCTRINE OF JESUS CHRIST, TEACHING THAT HE HAD A HUMAN SOUL AND THAT HE ONLY DIED FOR THE SINS OF THE "ELECT". THEY ALSO CLAIM TO BELIEVE IN SALVATION BY GRACE THROUGH THE BLOOD OF JESUS CHRIST, BUT THAT GRACE IS ONLY OFFERED TO THE "ELECT". THEY ARE A FALSE DENOMINATION THAT ALSO HAS THE DOCTRINAL ERRORS OF INFANT BAPTISM, THE UNIVERSAL CHURCH, THE SACRAMENTS AS "SIGNS AND SEALS", AND A GENERAL JUDGMENT.

---

(1) <u>Brief Outline of RCA History</u>, https://www.rca.org/about/history/

(2) <u>Belgic Confession</u>, https://www.crcna.org/welcome/beliefs/confessions/belgic-confession

(3) <u>What is the Reformed Church, and what do they believe?</u> https://www.gotquestions.org/Reformed-church.html

(4) <u>Bible Translations</u>, https://www.crcna.org/welcome/beliefs/bible-translations

(5) <u>How does the RCA practice baptism?</u>, https://www.rca.org/about/worship/baptism/

DENOMINATIONS-Lesson 25

Roman Catholic

Mark 7:5-9

Origin: "The Roman Catholic Church is built on the assumption that in Matthew 16:13-19 Jesus appointed Peter the first pope and so founded His Church and established the papacy." (1) (The True Church) "Cyprian [200-258, bishop of Carthage] was the first to establish clearly the distinction between the presbyters and bishops, and the primacy of the Roman church as the *Cathedra Petri*." [Chair of St. Peter] (2) (pg 266) "In 445, Leo, bishop of Rome…declared himself 'the pope'—that is, 'the father'—of all Christians on earth. Leo's claim was disputed by many in the church. In fact, it was not until 590 that Gregory, bishop of Rome, firmly established himself as pope." (3) (pg 28) About 1054 the Eastern Orthodox Church split from the Roman Catholic Church. The Reformation, sparked by Martin Luther in 1517, resulted in the formation of many 'protestant' denominations from Roman Catholic roots. Membership of the Roman Catholic Church is over 82 million in the U.S. and 1.3 billion worldwide. About half of those that call themselves Christian are Roman Catholic.

Doctrinal Beliefs:

1. The Bible

A. "105 God is the author of Sacred Scripture. 106 God inspired the human authors of the sacred books." (4)

B. "82 …Both Scripture and Tradition must be accepted and honoured with equal sentiments of devotion and reverence." (4)

C. "100 The task of interpreting the Word of God authentically has been entrusted solely to the Magisterium of the Church, that is, to the Pope and to the bishops in communion with him." (4)

D. "The New American Bible is a Roman Catholic Translation."(from the Preface to the Revised Edition of 1986-pg xviii) This translation leaves out 394 words of Jesus that are in the King James Bible!

E. Proof text: <u>Mark 7:7-8</u>

2. Salvation

A. "15 The second part of the Catechism explains how God's salvation, accomplished once for all through Christ Jesus and the Holy Spirit, is made present in the sacred actions of the Church liturgy...especially in the seven sacraments..." (4)

B. "1113...There are seven sacraments in the Church: Baptism, Confirmation or Chrismation, Eucharist, Penance, Anointing of the Sick, Holy Orders, and Matrimony." (4)

C. "1129 The Church affirms that for believers the sacraments of the New Covenant are necessary for salvation." (4)

D. "845 Outside the Church there is no salvation" "846...Basing itself on Scripture and Tradition...the Church...is necessary for salvation...Hence they could not be saved who, knowing that the Catholic Church was founded as necessary by God...would refuse...to enter it..." (4)

E. "969 ...Mary...by her manifold intercessions continues to bring us the gifts of eternal salvation." (4)

F. Proof texts: <u>Ephesians 2:8-9</u>, <u>Romans 10:3-4</u>

3. Baptism

A. "1213 Through Baptism we are freed from sin and reborn as sons of God; we become members of Christ." (4)

B. "1127...the sacraments confer the grace that they signify. They are efficacious because in them Christ himself is at work: it is he who baptizes, he who acts in the sacraments..." (4)

C. "Baptism of Infants 1250 Born with a fallen human nature and tainted by original sin, children also have need of the new birth in Baptism." (4)

D. "1239 Baptism is performed...by triple immersion...However, from ancient times it has also been able to be conferred by pouring the water three times over the candidate's head." (4)

E. Proof Text: <u>Titus 3:5</u>

4. The Church

A. "752 In Christian usage, the word 'church' designates the liturgical assembly, but also the local community or the whole universal community of believers." "779 The Church is...a hierarchical society and the Mystical Body of Christ." (4)

B. "870 The sole Church of Christ which in the Creed we profess to be one, holy, catholic, and apostolic...subsists in the Catholic Church, which is governed by the successor of Peter and by the bishops..." (4)

C. "963 ...Mary, Mother of Christ, Mother of the Church. 969 ...Therefore, the Blessed Virgin is invoked in the Church under the titles of Advocate, Helper, Benefactress, and Mediatrix." (4)

D. "882 The Pope, Bishop of Rome and Peter's successor...by reason of his office as Vicar of Christ, and as pastor of the entire Church has full, supreme and universal power over the whole Church, a power which he can always exercise unhindered." (4)

E. Proof Texts: <u>Ephesians 5:23</u>, <u>Matthew 12:46-50</u>, <u>Acts 20:28</u>

5. Jesus Christ

A. "I believe in Jesus Christ, his only Son, our Lord. He was conceived by the power of the Holy Spirit and born of the Virgin Mary. Under Pontius Pilate He was crucified, died, and was buried. He descended to the dead. On the third day he rose again. He ascended into heaven and is seated at the right hand of the Father. He will come again to judge the living and the dead." (4) (Apostles Creed)

B. "964 Mary's role in the Church is inseparable from her union with Christ... 'This union of the mother with the Son in the work of salvation'...in keeping with the divine plan, enduring with her only begotten Son the intensity of his suffering, joining herself with his sacrifice..." (4)

C. Proof Text: <u>I Timothy 2:5-6</u>

6. The Trinity (Godhead)

A. "233 Christians are baptized in the name of the Father and of the Son and of the Holy Spirit...for there is only one God, the almighty Father, his only Son and the Holy Spirit; the Most Holy Trinity." (4)

B. "971 The Church's devotion to the Blessed Virgin is intrinsic to Christian worship...to whose protection the faithful fly in all their dangers and needs... This very special devotion...differs essentially from the adoration which is given to the incarnate Word and equally to the Father and the Holy Spirit" (4)

C. Proof Texts: <u>II Corinthians 1:21-22</u>

7. Heaven And Hell

A. "1030 All who die in God's grace and friendship, but still imperfectly purified, are indeed assured of their eternal salvation; but after death they undergo purification...to achieve the holiness necessary to enter...heaven." (4)

B. "1031 The church gives the name Purgatory to this final purification of the elect, which is entirely different from the punishment of the damned...before the final judgment, there is a purifying fire." "1032 This teaching is also based on the practice of prayer for the dead..." (4)

C. "1035 ...the souls of those who die in a state of mortal sin descend into hell, where they suffer the punishments of hell, 'eternal fire'. The chief punishment of hell is eternal separation from God..." (4)

D. Proof text: <u>Luke 16:22-24</u>

THE ROMAN CATHOLIC RELIGION HAS A SALVATION BASED ON WORKS AND CEREMONIES AND THE FALSE DOCTRINE THAT MARY WAS A CO-SUFFERER AND IS A "MEDIATRIX" WITH JESUS CHRIST. THESE AND MANY OTHER ERRORS CAUSE ME TO CLASSIFY THIS GROUP IS A FALSE DENOMINATION.

---

(1) <u>Scriptural Truths for Roman Catholics</u>, pamphlet, Bartholomew F. Brewer,

https://comingintheclouds.org/about-catholic/catholic-doctrine/scriptural-truths-for-roman-catholics/

(2) <u>A Manual of Church History</u>, Vol. 1, Albert Henry Newman, Judson Press, Valley Forge, 1902, 1931, 1972.

(3) <u>So, What's the Difference?</u>, Fritz Ridenour, G/L Regal Books, a division of G/L Publications, Glendale, California, 1967.

(4) <u>CATECHISM OF THE CATHOLIC CHURCH</u>, http://www.vatican.va/archive/ENG0015/_INDEX.HTM

DENOMINATIONS-Lesson 26

Salvation Army

Origin: "The Salvation Army's beginnings date back to July 2, 1865 when a Methodist minister commenced a work in East London that would encircle the world before the end of the 19th century. It began as the Christian Revival Society and soon after was called the East London Christian Mission. William Booth, the founder of The Salvation Army, preached the Gospel to the poor and underprivileged and by 1867 it had developed into a ministry offering basic schooling, reading rooms, penny banks, soup kitchens, and relief aid to the destitute." (1) "Countries where the Salvation Army is at work-133...Corps-based community development programmes: 46,934...corps, out-posts, societies, new plants and recovery churches-14,703...Soldiers worldwide-1,250,413" (2) (About Us / International Statistics-2023 Yearbook)

Doctrinal Beliefs:

1. The Bible

A. "We believe that the Scriptures of the Old and New Testaments were given by inspiration of God, and that they only constitute the Divine rule of Christian faith and practice." (2) (Our Faith/Our Beliefs)

B. All Scripture quotes found were from the New International Version (NIV)

C. "...the NIV removed the word *Hell* in 40 out of 53 places (75%) it is found in the King James Bible." (3) (pg 296)

D. These six NIV passages remove references to Jesus' deity. (Luke 2:33, John 6:69, Romans 14:10-12, Ephesians 3:9, I Timothy 3:16 and I John 5:7-8)

E. Proof text: Revelation 22:18-19

2. Salvation

A. "We believe that the Lord Jesus Christ has by His suffering and death made an atonement for the whole world so that whosoever will may be saved." (2) (Our Faith/Our Beliefs)

B. "We believe that we are justified by grace through faith in our Lord Jesus Christ and that he that believeth hath the witness in himself." (2) (Our Faith/Our Beliefs)

C. "We believe that continuance in a state of salvation depends upon continued obedient faith in Christ." (2) (Our Faith/Our Beliefs)

D. "We believe that it is the privilege of all believers to be 'wholly sanctified'...." (2) (Our Faith/Our Beliefs) ["Whole" or "entire" sanctification is a Methodist doctrine which states that sometime after salvation a person receives the baptism of the Holy Spirit. At that time the person is supposedly indwelt by the Holy Spirit and made free from original sin.]

E. Proof texts: John 6:39-40, Romans 8:9

3. Baptism

A. "We hear our Lord's command to make disciples, baptising them in the name of the Father, the Son and the Holy Spirit. We believe that soldiership is discipleship and that the public swearing-in of a soldier of The Salvation Army beneath the Army's trinitarian flag fulfills this command. It is a public response and witness to the life-changing encounter with Christ which has already taken place, as is the believer's water baptism practised by some other Christians. (4) (Pg 305, Soldiership) [swearing in replaces baptism]

B. "The Salvation Army has never said it is wrong to use sacraments, nor does it deny that other Christians receive grace from God through using them...The reasons for The Salvation Army's cessation of the sacraments may be summarised as follows...3. The sacraments had been a divisive influence in the Church throughout Christian history...4. Some churches would not allow women to administer the sacraments." (5)

C. Proof Text: Acts 2:41, 10:47-48

4. The Church

A. Founder William Booth said, "We came into this position originally by determining not to be a Church. We did not wish to undertake the administration of the Sacraments, and thereby bring ourselves into collision with existing Churches." (6) Booth determined NOT to be a Church!

B. But in 2010 they wrote: "WE BELIEVE that The Salvation Army is an international Christian church...and is an integral part of the Body of Christ like other Christian churches, and that the Army's local corps are local congregations like the local congregations of other Christian churches." (4) (The Army's Identity, Pg 316)

C. "Booth's wife, Catherine, was a brilliant preacher and played a leading role in determining The Salvation Army's direction and doctrines; she became known as The Army's Mother. From the beginning, Catherine Booth firmly established equality for women to be ordained ministers of the gospel and to hold leadership positions within The Salvation Army. (1)

D. "The International Headquarters of the Salvation Army is located in London... since 1881...houses the offices of the General of the Salvation Army and the Chief of Staff. The international headquarters...'oversees, coordinates and supports the work' of the Salvation Army in its 133 countries.." (7)

E. Proof Texts: <u>II Corinthians 8:1</u>, <u>1 Timothy 3:1-2</u>

5. Jesus Christ

A. "We believe that in the person of Jesus Christ the Divine and human natures are united, so that He is truly and properly God and truly and properly man." (2) (Our Faith/Our Beliefs)

B. "We believe that the Lord Jesus Christ has by His suffering and death made an atonement for the whole world, so that whosoever will may be saved" (2) (Our Faith/Our Beliefs)

C. Proof Text: <u>Philippians 2:5-11</u>

6. The Trinity (Godhead)

A. "We believe that there are three persons in the Godhead-the Father, the Son and the Holy Ghost, undivided in essence and co-equal in power and glory." (2) (Our Faith/Our Beliefs)

B. Proof Texts: <u>Acts 10:38</u>

7. Heaven And Hell

A. "We believe in the immortality of the soul; the resurrection of the body; the general judgment at the end of the world; the eternal happiness of the righteous; and the endless punishment of the wicked." (2) (Our Faith/Our Beliefs)

B. Proof texts: <u>John 5:28-29</u>, <u>Revelation 20:4-6</u>

THIS GROUP HAS A CORRECT DOCTRINE OF JESUS CHRIST BUT ERR IN THE TEACHING OF "ENTIRE SANCTIFICATION" AND "CONTINUED OBEDIENT FAITH IN CHRIST" AS NECESSARY FOR SALVATION, MAKING THEM A FALSE DENOMINA-TION. THEY ALSO BELIEVE IN THE "UNIVERSAL CHRISTIAN CHURCH" AND A "GENERAL JUDGMENT".

---

(1) <u>Our History, English Beginnings</u>, http://www.salvos.org.au/about-us/our-history/foundation-in-london.php

(2) <u>The Salvation Army International</u>, https://www.salvationarmy.org/

(3) <u>Final Authority</u>, William P. Grady, Grady Publications, Schererville, Indiana, 1993.

(4) <u>The Salvation Army Handbook Of Doctrine</u>, Published by Salvation Books, The Salvation Army International Headquarters, 101 Queen Victoria Street, London EC4V 4EH, United Kingdom, This edition published 2010

(5) <u>Why does The Salvation Army not baptise or hold communion?</u>,

http://www.histonsalvationarmy.co.uk/2009/index.php?option=com_content&view=article&id=418:why-does-the-salvation-army-not-baptise-or-hold communion&catid =25:what-are-we-about&Itemid=59

(6) <u>The Life of General William Booth</u>, Chapter 28, Pages 468-469. https://archive.org/stream/lifeofgeneralwil01begbuoft/lifeofgeneralwil01begbuoft_djvu.tt

(7) <u>International Headquarters of The Salvation Army</u>, https://en.wikipedia.org/wiki/International_Headquarters_of_The_Salvation_Army

DENOMINATIONS-Lesson 27

Scientology

Origin: "The word Scientology literally means 'the study of truth'." (1) "Scientology is a set of beliefs and practices invented by the American author L. Ron Hubbard...By 1954 he had...founded the Church of Scientology...Prominent celebrities who have joined the Church include John Travolta, Tom Cruise, Kirstie Alley, Nancy Cartwright, and Juliette Lewis...As of 2016, scholarly estimates suggest that there are a maximum of 40,000 Scientologists...They are found mostly in the U.S., Europe, South Africa and Australia." (2)

Doctrinal Beliefs:

1. The Bible

A. "...Scientologist's...do not regard the Bible as the inspired Word of God and do not believe what the Word teaches. (3)

B. "Hubbard lies at the core of Scientology, with his writings remaining the source of its doctrines and practices...He published hundreds of articles and books over the course of his life, writings that Scientologists regard as scripture" (2)

C. Proof Texts: Joshua 1:8, Psalms 119:9, 11

2. Salvation

A. "Scientologists do not see the need for Jesus as Savior since they basically believe mankind is good and not evil...they don't need a Savior because sin is just a lack of intelligence or knowledge...By rejecting Jesus as Savior, they do not pursue the only possible way to gain eternal life " (3)

B. "Salvation is achieved through the practices and techniques of Scientology, the ultimate goal of which is to realize one's true nature as an immortal spirit, a thetan. The path to salvation, or enlightenment, includes achieving states of increasingly greater mental awareness—Pre-Clear, Clear, and ultimately Operating Thetan. An Operating Thetan is a spirit who can control matter, energy, space, time, thought, and life." (4) (Salvation)

C. Proof Texts: <u>Ephesians 2:2-3, 8-9</u>, <u>Ecclesiastes 12:7</u>

3. Baptism

A. "Naming Ceremony-This is a form of Baptism." (5)

B. "The Church's naming ceremony for infants is designed to help orient a thetan in its new body and introduce it to its godparents. During the ceremony, the minister reminds the child's parents and godparents of their duty to assist the newly reborn thetan and to encourage it towards spiritual freedom." (2)

C. Proof Texts: <u>Matthew 28:19-20</u>

4. The Church

> A. "Worship Services-Each Sunday, and sometimes on other days of the week as well, the Church's Chaplain or another minister conducts a public worship service which is open to both members and non-members of the Church. These services comprise a recitation of the Creed of Scientology, sermons, congregational auditing and prayer.

Ceremonies-In addition Scientology congregations celebrate weddings and namings with their own formal ceremonies and mark the passing of their fellows with funeral rites." (6) (No Bible used!)

B. "Women are able to become ministers and rise through the Church ranks in the same manner as men." (2)

C. Proof Texts: <u>Matthew 16:18</u>, <u>Revelation 1:10-11</u>

5. Jesus Christ

A. "Jesus is described inconsistently, and mostly unfavorably, by L. Ron Hubbard the founder of Scientology. In early writings and lectures, Hubbard considered Jesus merely a teacher in his time, but later Hubbard described Jesus and the Crucifixion as fictitious. In later material by Hubbard in which he claimed himself to be both Maitreya Buddha and the Antichrist, Hubbard said his own mission in the world was to prevent the Second Coming of Christ and went on to describe Jesus as a 'lover of young boys' and given to 'uncontrollable bursts of temper and hatred.'" (7) (Hubbard's views of Jesus)

B. "There are no particular human incarnations of God, as the universal life force (Theta) is inherent in all. All humans are immortal spiritual beings (thetans) capable of realizing a nearly godlike state through Scientology practices." (4) (Incarnations)

C. "They do not believe that Jesus is God... They believe that He was a good teacher who never quite reached a high enough spiritual awareness. " (3)

D. Proof Texts: I John 4:1-6

6. The Trinity (Godhead)

A. "They don't believe in God as the Creator of human life because humans were supposed to come from another planet...the "'parent planet.'" (3)

B. "Scientology refers to the existence of a Supreme Being, but practitioners are not expected to worship it. No intercessions are made to seek this Being's assistance in daily life." (2)

C. "The nature of the Supreme Being is revealed personally through each individual as s/he becomes more conscious and spiritually aware. There exists a life energy or force (Theta) beyond and within all." (4) (Belief in Deity)

D. Proof Texts: Luke 3:21-22

7. Heaven And Hell

A. "Rebirths continue until one consciously confronts all pre-birth, current-life, and previous-life traumas and realizes one's true nature as a 'thetan,' immortal spirit—transcending matter, energy, space, and time. Achieving this state enables the spirit to escape the cycle of birth and death—to operate independently of the physical universe and become one with God." (4) (After Death)

B. "Their belief of the afterlife is that humans are immortal and really never die and that this 'immortal spiritual being' has lived another life before and will live another life again. This means that they have lived many lives before and will live other lives after death and will continue to do so for all eternity." (3)

C. Proof Texts: <u>Luke 16:19-24</u>

SCIENTOLOGY IS DEFINITELY A FALSE DENOMINATION, TEACHING THERE WAS NO DIVINE INCARNATION OF JESUS CHRIST AND SALVATION BY REINCARNATION UNTIL "ACHIEVING STATES OF INCREASINGLY GREATER MENTAL AWARENESS".

---

(1) <u>Introduction To Scientology</u>, https://www.scientologyboise.org/about-us/

(2) <u>Scientology</u>, http://en.wikipedia.org/wiki/Scientology

(3) <u>What Is Scientology? What Do They Believe? Are They Christian?</u>, https://www.whatchristianswanttoknow.com/what-is-scientology-what-do-they-believe-are-they-christian/

(4) <u>What Do Scientologists Believe?</u>, http://www.beliefnet.com/faiths/scientology/what- do-scientologists-believe.aspx

(5) <u>Scientology</u>, by James R. Lewis, Published by Oxford University Press, 198 Madison Avenue, New York, New York 10016, 2009

(6) <u>SCIENTOLOGY RELIGIOUS CEREMONIES</u>, https://www.scientology.org/what-is-scientology/scientology-religious-ceremonies/

(7) <u>Scientology and religious groups</u>, https://en.wikipedia.org/wiki/Scientology_and_ religious_groups

DENOMINATIONS-Lesson 28

Seventh-Day Adventist

Jeremiah 14:14

Origin: "The Seventh-day Adventist Church[a] is an Adventist Protestant Christian denomination which is distinguished by its observance of Saturday, the seventh day of the week in the Christian (Gregorian) and the Hebrew calendar, as the Sabbath, its emphasis on the imminent Second Coming (advent) of Jesus Christ, and its annihilationist soteriology. The denomination grew out of the Millerite movement in the United States during the mid-19th century and it was formally established in 1863. Among its co-founders was Ellen G. White, whose extensive writings are still held in high regard by the church." (1) (Introduction) "...the theology of William Miller differed from Seventh-Day Adventist theology in three distinct points: he denied the Seventh-day Sabbath...the sleep of the soul...the final, utter destruction of the wicked...And he never embraced the 'sanctuary' and 'investigative judgment' theories developed by Seventh-Day Adventists." (2) (pg 363) "The Seventh-day Adventist Church is one of the world's fastest-growing organizations, primarily from membership increases in developing nations. Today much of the church membership reside outside of the United States, with large numbers in Africa, Asia and Latin America... In 2019 the Seventh-day Adventist Church had 21,000,000 baptized members around the world... In 2021, the Seventh-day Adventist Church had 1.2 million members worshiping in Canada and the United States" (1) (Membership) General Conference headquarters are in Silver Springs, Maryland.

Doctrinal Beliefs:

1. The Bible

A. "1. Holy Scriptures-The Holy Scriptures, Old and New Testaments, are the written Word of God, given by divine inspiration. The inspired authors spoke and wrote as they were moved by the Holy Spirit...The Holy Scriptures are the ...infallible revelation of His will." (3)

B. "18. The Gift Of Prophecy-...This gift is an identifying mark of the remnant church and we believe it was manifested in the ministry of Ellen G. White. Her writings speak with prophetic authority and provide comfort, guidance, instruction, and correction to the church." (3) (continuing revelation in prophesy)

C. Proof texts: II Peter 1:20-21, II Timothy 3:16-17

2. Salvation

A. "10. The Experience Of Salvation-...Led by the Holy spirit we sense our need, acknowledge our sinfulness, repent of our transgressions, and exercise faith in Jesus as our Saviour and Lord...This saving faith comes through the divine power of the Word and is the gift of God's grace...we are born again and sanctified...we are given the power to live a holy life..." (3)

B. "One who truly understands and accepts the teachings of the Seventh Day Adventist Church can assuredly know that he is born again, and that he is fully accepted by the Lord." (4) (pg 105)

C. "...the acceptance of Christ at conversion does not seal a person's destiny. His life record after conversion is also important. A man may go back on his repentance, or by careless inattention let slip the very life he has espoused. Nor can it be said that a man's record is closed when he comes to the end of his days. He is responsible for his influence during life, and is just as surely responsible for his evil influence after he is dead." (4) (pg 420)

D. Proof texts: I Thessalonians 5:23, II Corinthians 5:8, Titus 1:2

3. Baptism

A. "15. Baptism-By baptism we confess our faith in the death and resurrection of Jesus Christ...and are received as members by His church." (3)

B. "Seventh-day Adventists do not believe in baptizing infants. A person must be old enough to accept responsibility for his/her own actions. Baptism is by immersion. In order to be baptized, a person must agree to this set of thirteen baptismal VOWS:" (5) (Summarized they are: [1] belief in the Trinity, [2] acceptance and faith in Jesus Christ for salvation, [3] renouncing the world and sin, [4] accept the righteousness of Christ to live a godly life, [5] believe the Bible is God's Word, [6] accept 10 commandments as binding, including keeping the sabbath, [7] looking for the soon coming of Jesus, [8] accept gift of prophecy as identifying mark of the remnant church, [9] purpose to give tithes and offerings to the church, [10] abstain from unclean foods and harmful substances, [11] live in harmony with the principles of the Seventh-day Adventist Church, [12] be baptized as a public profession of salvation, [13] accept the Seventh-day Church as the remnant church of Bible prophecy.)

C. Proof Text: <u>Acts 8:35-39</u>

4. The Church

A. "13. The Remnant And Its Mission-The universal church is composed of all who truly believe in Christ...a remnant has been called out" (3)

B. "The world church is governed by a General Conference[1], with smaller regions administered by divisions, union conferences and local conferences." (2)

C. "The name Seventh-day Adventist is based on the Church's observance of the 'biblical Sabbath' on Saturday, the seventh day of the week. 'Advent' means *coming* and refers to their belief that Jesus Christ will soon return to this earth." (6) (Introduction)

D. Proof Texts: <u>Galatians 1:2 & 22</u>

5. Jesus Christ

A. "4. God the Son (Jesus Christ)-God the eternal Son became incarnate in Jesus Christ. Through Him all things were created...He was conceived of the Holy Spirit and born of the virgin Mary...He suffered and died voluntarily on the cross for our sins and in our place. He will come again in glory..." (3)

B. "3. Christ's Ministry in the Heavenly Sanctuary-In 1844...He (Jesus) entered the second and last phase of His atoning ministry...by the cleansing of the

---

1. http://en.wikipedia.org/wiki/General_Conference_of_Seventh-day_Adventists

ancient Hebrew sanctuary on the Day of Atonement...with the perfect sacrifice of the blood of Jesus." (3)

C. Proof Text: <u>Acts 2:22-24</u>

6. The Trinity (Godhead)

A. "2. The Trinity- There is one God: Father, Son, and Holy Spirit, a unity of three coeternal Persons." (3)

B. Proof Text: <u>Hebrews 9:14</u>

7. Heaven And Hell

A. "Adventists believe that...(in 1844), Christ went into the most holy place to cleanse it before his second coming on Earth...His work in the heavenly sanctuary is a work of investigative judgment which reveals which of the dead are righteous and should be resurrected at the second coming, and which of the living are worthy of Heaven. Those who pretended to be followers of God, but whose lives were not righteous, will be discovered by this investigation." (6) (Beliefs-The Heavenly Sanctuary)

B. "26. Death and Resurrection-Until that day death is an unconscious state for all people." (3)

C. "25. The Second Coming Of Christ-...the righteous dead will be resurrected and together with the righteous living will be...taken to heaven..." (3)

D. "27. The Millennium And The End Of Sin-...the thousand-year reign of Christ with His saints in heaven between the first and second resurrections. During this time the wicked dead will be judged; the earth will be...without living human inhabitants, but occupied by Satan and his angels. At its close...the unrighteous dead will then be resurrected...fire from God will consume them and cleanse the earth." (3)

E. "We reject the doctrine of eternal torment..." (4) (page 543)

F. Proof text: <u>Revelation 14:10-11</u>

THIS GROUP IS A FALSE DENOMINATION. IT HAS AN INCORRECT DOCTRINE OF JESUS CHRIST, SAYING THAT HIS ATONEMENT FOR OUR SINS CONTINUED AFTER HIS ASCENSION IN THE "HEAVENLY SANCTUARY". THEY ALSO TEACH THAT SALVATION IS BASED ON ACCEPTING "THE TEACHINGS OF THE SEVENTH-DAY ADVENTIST CHURCH", "CONTINUING TO LIVE A HOLY LIFE" AND NOT GOING "BACK ON YOUR REPENTANCE".

---

(1) Seventh-day Adventist Church, http://en.wikipedia.org/wiki/Seventh-day Adventist Church

(2) The Kingdom of the Cults, Walter Martin, Bethany Fellowship, Inc., Publishers,

Minneapolis, Minnesota, 1965, 1977

(3) 28 Fundamental Beliefs, 2015 Edition, General Conference of Seventh-day Adventists ®, 12501 Old Columbia Pike, Silver Spring, MD 20904, USA 301-680-6000

http://www.adventist.org/beliefs/fundamental/index.html

(4) Seventh-day Adventists Answer Questions On Doctrine, Copyright 1957, Review and Herald Publishing Association, Washington, D.C., may be viewed online at: http://www.sdanet.org/atissue/books/qod/

(5) Official SDA Baptismal Vows (13), https://www.bible.ca/cr-SDA#baptism

(6) BBC Seventh-day Adventists, https://www.bbc.co.uk/religion/religions/christianity/ subdivisions/ seventhdayadventist_1.shtml

DENOMINATIONS-Lesson 29

Shinto

Origin: "The term Shinto in English comes from two Japanese words, 'shin' (which can also be read kami, meaning gods) and 'to'...meaning 'way'...Shinto is translated best as 'The Divine Way.'" (1)(page 1) "Shinto is an ancient Japanese religion. Starting about 500 BCE[1] (or earlier) it was originally an amorphous mix of nature worship, fertility cults, divination techniques, hero worship, and shamanism...in the 8th Century C.E[2]., At that time, The Yamato dynasty consolidated its rule over most of Japan. Divine origins were ascribed to the imperial family. Shinto established itself as an official religion of Japan, along with Buddhism[3]. The complete separation of Japanese religion from politics did not occur until just after World War II." (2) (Brief history of Shinto) "Before 1946 Shinto took two forms: State, or Shrine, Shinto, a patriotic nationalistic cult, identified with and financially supported by the imperial government; and Sectarian Shinto, a general term for a number of sects founded by private people and based on various interpretations of traditional Shinto...during the American occupation of Japan following World War II, the cult was completely separated from the state by order of General Douglas MacArthur, supreme commander for the Allied powers. Government financial support of State Shinto was eliminated, the former practice of teaching cult doctrines in the schools was abolished, and the use of Shinto symbols for nationalistic purposes was forbidden. At the same time the emperor issued a statement renouncing all claims to divinity...Sectarian Shinto, a religion of the same status as Buddhism and Christianity, was unaffected by these changes...In the mid-1990s 110 million Japanese participated in the various Shinto sects, but those who professed Shinto as their sole or major religion numbered only 3.4 million." (3)(III. Contemporary Shinto) "One source estimates 1000 followers of Shinto in North America. The Canadian Census (1991) recorded only 445 in

---

1. http://www.religioustolerance.org/bce.htm

2. http://www.religioustolerance.org/ce.htm

3. http://www.religioustolerance.org/buddhism.htm

Canada." (2) (Number of Adherents) "Shinto is a deeply held religious belief and attitude toward life held by nearly all the people of Japan." (1)(page 6)

Doctrinal Beliefs:

1. The Bible

A. "Many texts are valued in the Shinto religion. Most date from the 8th century CE: the Kojiki (Record of Ancient Matters); the Rokkukushi (Six National Histories); the Shoku Nihongi or Nihon Shoki (Continuing Chronicles of Japan); and the Jinno Shotiki (a study of Shinto and Japanese politics and history) was written in the 14th century." (2) (Shinto Texts)

B. "Unlike most other religions, Shinto has no real founder, no written scriptures, no body of religious law, and only a very loosely-organized priesthood." (2) (Brief history of Shinto)

C. The Bible is never referred to in the Shinto religion.

D. Proof texts: <u>Psalms 119:97-105, John 17:14a & 17</u>

2. Salvation

A. "All of humanity is regarded as 'Kami's child'. Thus all human life...is sacred. Believers revere 'musuhi', the Kamis' creative and harmonizing powers. They aspire to have 'makoto', sincerity or true heart..." (2) (Shinto Beliefs)

B. "There are 'Four Affirmations' in Shinto: 1. *Tradition and the family*...2. *Love of nature*: Nature is sacred; to be in contact with nature is to be close to the gods. Natural objects are worshipped as sacred spirits...3. *Physical cleanliness*...4. '*Matsuri*'" (this festival honors the Kami and ancestral spirits) (2) (Shinto beliefs)

C. "Shinto teaches that by a priest waving a purification wand and the washing of the mouth and finger tips with plain water a person can be purified of unrighteousness (Ono, 51-52)." (1)(page 5)

D. Proof text: <u>Romans 10:9-13</u>

3. Baptism

A. "In the past, believers practiced 'misogi', the washing of their bodies in a river near the shrine. In recent years they only wash their hands and wash out their mouths in a wash basin provided within the shrine grounds." (2) (Shinto Practices)

B. They do not practice any form of baptism.

C. Proof Text: <u>Acts 8:12</u>

4. The Church

A. "Shinto recognizes many sacred places: mountains, springs, etc...Each shrine is dedicated to a specific Kami who has a divine personality and responds to sincere prayers of the faithful. When entering a shrine, one passes through a 'Tori', a special gateway for the Gods. it marks the demarcation between the finite world and the infinite world of the Gods...Shrine ceremonies, which include cleansing, offerings, prayers, and dances are directed to the Kami." (2) (Shinto Practices)

B. "Followers are expected to visit Shinto shrines at the times of various life passages. For example, the *Shichigosan Matsuri* involves a blessing by the shrine Priest of girls aged 3 and 7, and boys aged 5. It is held on NOV-15." (2) (Shinto Practices)

C. Proof Text: <u>Matthew 16:18</u>

5. Jesus Christ

A. "Shinto creation stories tell of the history and lives of the "Kami" (deities). Among them was a divine couple, Izanagi-no-mikoto and Izanami-no-mikoto, who gave birth to the Japanese islands. Their children became the deities of the various Japanese clans." (2) (Shinto Beliefs)

B. "Shingo bills itself as 'Kirisuto no Sato', which translates as 'Hometown of Christ', and it has developed an amazing mythology...According to this mythology, it was not Jesus who was crucified at Golgotha; it was his brother.

Jesus did what any man who had been marked for crucifixion would do. He left the area as quickly as possible! Apparently he headed north and then east across Siberia until he reached Japan, where he changed his name to Daitenku Taro Jurai. As soon as he settled down, he did what most committed immigrants to Japan do: he married a local girl and raised a family. The girl he is supposed to have married was called Miyuko, and she bore him three daughters. Apparently, this arrangement suited him so well that he lived to the amazing age of 106, which is much longer than he would have lived had he stayed in the Middle East or headed west into Europe. This astonishing story of Christ's miraculous flight to Japan germinated in 1935, when a Shinto priest found some ancient scrolls that told the tale. After World War II, the people of Shingo realized that the discovery of Christ's tomb could have enormous economic benefits. Consequently, the myth really took off..." (4)

C. "In 1867...According to revived Shinto doctrine, the sovereignty of the emperor was exercised by divine right through his reputed descent from the sun goddess Amaterasu Omikami, who is considered the founder of the Japanese nation. (3)(II. Early History)

D. Shinto has no official doctrine concerning Jesus Christ.

E. Proof Text: <u>I John 5:10-12</u>

6. The Trinity (Godhead)

A. "The Sun Goddess is regarded as the chief deity. There are numerous other deities...They are seen as benign; they sustain and protect. There are no concepts which compare to the Christian beliefs in the wrath of God, His omnipotence and omni-presence, or the separation of God from humanity due to sin." (2)(Shinto Beliefs)

B. "One area of great difficulty between Christianity and Shinto is the Shinto belief in *kami* -- many 'gods'—instead of in the one true God, the Holy Trinity. (1)(page 5)

C. Proof Text: <u>John 1:1-3</u>

7. Heaven And Hell

A. "Their religious texts discuss the 'High Plain of Heaven' and the 'Dark Land' which is an unclean land of the dead, but give few details." (2)(Shinto Beliefs)

B. Proof text: <u>Daniel 12:1-3</u>

THIS RELIGION IS OBVIOUSLY AN FALSE DENOMINATION WITHOUT JESUS CHRIST AND DEPENDING ON "SINCERITY" OR A "TRUE HEART" OR CLEANSING BY A PRIEST FOR SALVATION.

---

(1) <u>SHINTO, "THE WAY OF THE GODS," OR JESUS CHRIST, GOD'S "WAY"?</u>

by Richard S. Lofgren, http://ctsfw.net/media/pdfs/lofgrenshinto.pdf

(2) <u>What Is Shinto?</u>, http://www.japanhemp.org/en/shintoinfo.htm

(3) <u>Philosophy of Religion, Chapter 2, Religions of the World, Section 7, Shintoism</u>, http://www.qcc.cuny.edu/SocialSciences/ppecorino/PHIL_of_RELIGION_TEXT/CH APTER_2_RELIGIONS/Shintoism.htm

(4) <u>The Last Journey of Jesus Christ</u>[4], Charles R. Pringle, 2007

http://chapan.wordpress.com/2007/03/03/the-last-journey-of-jesus-christ/

---

4. http://chapan.wordpress.com/2007/03/03/the-last-journey-of-jesus-christ/

DENOMINATIONS-Lesson 30

Two by Two's (Christian Conventions)

<u>Matthew 10:1-14</u>

Origin: "It was started by William Irvine, a Scotsman, who joined the Faith Mission established by a John Govan, in 1895. In 1896, Irvine was sent to Ireland for the mission and began canvassing for converts of his own the following year. By 1900 he had gained enough supporters to break away from the mission which had been supporting him up until this time. (Edward) Cooney joined Irvine who by this time had a number of followers, in 1901." (1)(The Founders) "This group claims that it takes no name...In 1942 the group registered as a church with the United States government using the name, 'Christian Conventions'...Those in the group refer to it as 'the Truth', or 'the Way' when talking amongst themselves. To outsiders this group is known as the Cooneyites after Eddie Cooney, one of their early preachers. Other names such as the "Go-preachers", the "Two by Twos" and so on, have also been attached to the group over the years." (1)(Taking No Name) "The group has about 200,000 members worldwide." (2) "It is very difficult...to get an official outline of their doctrines, for they purposely refrain from printing books or tracts for public circulation." (3)(Their Doctrines)

Doctrinal Beliefs:

1. The Bible

A. "I have quoted from the King James version of the Bible because this is the only version that the group allowed while I was in the fellowship." (1)(Reasons For writing This Book)

B. That Their Ministers "are God's only true ministers...are the supreme authorities in Biblical interpretation, have authority and rule over members, viewpoints are considered as authoritative as the written Word." (2)(How they differ from orthodox Christian beliefs-in what they believe)

C. "They...declare that the Bible is a 'Dead Book' unless it is 'made to live' through the mouth of one of their preachers. (3)(Their Doctrines)

D. "They do NOT believe conversion can take place through the written Word without human agency." (4)(4. What They Do Not Believe)

E. Proof texts: <u>II Peter 1:20</u>, <u>Hebrews 4:12</u>

2. Salvation

A. "The basic doctrine of this church, which claims to have no name, is that salvation is only possible through their homeless, itinerant, 'unsalaried', unmarried 'workers'." (5)(Doctrinal Heresies)

B. "Salvation is only possible through hearing 'their' Gospel, through 'their' workers'...Faith in Jesus alone is not enough...The workers' claim that one must follow them in order to be saved." (1)(The Ministry)

C. "Assert that everyone in the world is lost except themselves, yet have no assurance of their own salvation because they believe one cannot know whether one is saved until death because one can 'lose out' at any time." (5)(Scriptural Errors in Personal Life)

D. Proof texts: <u>I Corinthians 15:1-3</u>, <u>I John 5:11-13</u>

3. Baptism

A. "Those who had 'professed' during the year were baptised at convention. We had to put on some old ladies clothes and were required to wear old fashioned woollen togs that had been kept by 'the workers' for the occasion. We were taken to a spot where the creek had been banked up to make it deep enough for us to be baptised in. (1)(My Testimony)

B. "Their converts must be baptized by immersion" (3) (Method And Practices)

C. "Assert that baptism must be performed by specific workers to be considered valid. Workers decide who may be baptized." (5)(Errors Regarding The Church)

D. Proof Text: <u>Acts 2:41</u>

4. The Church

A. "The workers' claim that true believers must meet in homes like they did in the New Testament, referring to the church that was in the home of Aquila and Priscilla...This group holds 'meetings' in the homes of its followers on a Sunday morning. These are called 'fellowship meetings' and only members are allowed to attend, in contrast to Gospel meetings or missions which are held in rented halls for the purpose of gaining converts." (1)(The Church In The Home)

B. "Assert that it is unscriptural and wicked to build church buildings, yet they construct and maintain buildings on convention property, needed only eight days out of the year." (5)(Errors Regarding The Church)

C. "One of the foundational beliefs of the Friends & Worker's fellowship is the notion that its preachers (called "workers") most closely resemble the early Christians in the Bible because they travel two by two...workers travel in celibate pairs, staying in the homes of the 'Friends' - a male worker has a male companion worker with him, and likewise, a female worker has a female companion worker. Together they go out and preach, leading the worship services at conventions, gospel meetings, Sunday morning meetings, and in private bible studies." (6) "Assert that the 'workers' are 'apostles'. Twice as many women workers as men." (5)(Errors Regarding The Church)

D. Absolute authority in each region is exercised by a "head worker." Local itinerant workers employ similar power over the membership. Elders oversee the church in the absence of a worker." (5) (Doctrinal Heresies)

E. "That Salvation...is not possible without being in their fellowship." (2)(How they differ from orthodox Christian beliefs—in what they believe)

F. Proof Texts: <u>Ephesians 2:8-9</u>, <u>Philippians 1:1</u>

5. Jesus Christ

A. "They believe that Jesus came to be a perfect example; a pattern minister or way-shower...that Jesus' life is equal to or more important than His death." (2)(Regarding Jesus)

B. "The Jesus Way" of the Cooneyites, accordingly, has no room for the precious atoning blood of Christ as the ground of salvation...'How can the blood of a dead man save anyone?' Underlying that question is an assault upon both the deity and the atoning work of Christ." (3)(The Atoning Work Of Christ)

C. "The Go-Preachers profess to believe in the deity of Christ, but utterances such as this, 'Jesus overcame His own flesh", clearly show they believe that the Lord Jesus Christ had sinful flesh in Him that needed to be overcome!" (3)(What Think Ye Of Christ?)

D. "Most in this group seem unsure of who Jesus really is. They bring Him down to their level by claiming that He is 'our elder brother', 'our example or pattern preacher'. They preach that, 'Christ had a human nature, too. He was a man, God is our father and Jesus is our elder brother.' They do not preach that Jesus was Emmanuel – God with us, or God manifest in the flesh." (1)(The Deity Of Christ)

E. Proof Text: <u>I Peter 1:18-19</u>

6. The Trinity (Godhead)

A. They are "Ignorant of the biblical, Triune God: Three persons as one God... Antitrinitarian. Assert that only the Father is God...Assert that Jesus is not God...'Jesus is the Son of God, only a man, filled with the Spirit'...Assert that the Holy Spirit is not God, but simply a force or energy from God." (5)(Errors In The Concept Of God)

B. Proof Text: <u>I John 5:7-8</u>

7. Heaven And Hell

A. "Cooney's sermons were provocative and hostile toward existing churches, as he proclaimed that members of all other churches were doomed to hell." (7)

B. "All people either receive eternal life in heaven or eternal punishment in hell, depending upon their allowance of God's work in their life while on earth." (2)(Articles, Fact Sheet, After Life)

C. Proof text: <u>Titus 3:5</u>

THIS GROUP IS A FALSE RELIGION, TEACHING THAT JESUS CHRIST AND THE HOLY SPIRIT ARE NOT GOD. ALSO TEACHING THAT ONLY THEIR MEMBERS ARE SAVED.

---

(1) <u>The Church With No Name</u>, By Lynn Cooper, 1996, self-published by the author, ISBN 0-473-03810-2

(2) <u>Two-by-twos</u>, http://www.apologeticsindex.org/t17.html

(3) <u>The Cooneyites or "Go-Preachers" and their Doctrines</u>, Pamphlet, W.M. Rule, The Central Bible Truth Depot, London, England, 1917. https://www.tellingthetruth.info/publications_index/rulewm.php

(4) <u>Two-by-Two's or (2x2's)</u>, (This is not an official document, but compiled from former members of the group.) http://www.bible.ca/cr-2x2.htm

(5) <u>Facts You Should Know About The Christian Convention Church</u>, https://web.archive.org/web/20140614061144/http://www.culthelp.info:80/index.php?option=com_content&task=view&id=187&Itemid=8

(6) <u>Should Women be Workers?</u>, http://www.angelfire.com/ok3/apologia/women.html

(7) <u>Who are the Two by Twos and the Cooneyites, and what do they believe?</u> https://gotquestions.org/Two-by-Twos-Cooneyites.html

DENOMINATIONS-Lesson 31

Unification Church (Moonies)

M<u>atthew 24:4-5</u>

Origin: "Sun Myung Moon was born in 1920 in Korea...Around 1930, his parents became fervent Presbyterians...At Easter 1935...praying in the Korean mountains, Moon had a vision of Jesus, who asked him to continue the work Jesus had begun on earth nearly 2000 years before. On May 1, 1954, in Seoul, moon founded the Holy Spirit Association for the Unification of World Christianity, popularly called the Unification Church...In 1959, the first missionaries arrived in the United States...In 1971, Moon expanded his ministry by coming to the United States...In 1975...Moon sent missionaries to 120 countries...In the 1980's he was convicted of tax evasion and imprisoned in the U.S. for thirteen months." (1) (pg 329) "Moon has also launched numerous business ventures, and with the free labor of his followers, has built a multi-million dollar empire that includes pharmaceutical companies, manufacturing, banking, publishing, and other industries...They...publish a monthly magazine called *Insight*. While not an official publication of the Unification Church, the Church does own and operate the *Washington Times*" (2) "On 1 May 1994 (the 40th anniversary of the founding of the HSA-UWC), Moon declared that the era of the HSA-UWC had ended and inaugurated a new organization: the Family Federation for World Peace and Unification" (3) "The 28-year-old son of South Korea's Unification Church founder Sun Myung Moon...Reverend Hyung Jin Moon...became the Chairman of the Family Federation for World Peace and Unification...taking charge of the church's world and domestic organizations." (4)

Doctrinal Beliefs:

1. The Bible

A. "...the Bible is 'not the truth itself, but a textbook teaching the truth'. Moon's... *Divine Principle*, is considered to be their scriptures...revealed directly to Moon by Jesus Christ), along with the Bible. They...believe in continuing revelation. (Moon claims to have received new revelations from God; i.e., 'I spoke with Jesus Christ in the spirit world. And...with John the Baptist. This is my authority.')...Moon's interpretations and teachings are considered to be the final and absolute source of authority..." (2) (1. Source of Authority)

B. "Moon's book, *The Divine Principle*, was, he claims revealed to him over a period of 9 years after he claims Jesus appeared to him on Easter Sunday 1936...The *Divine Principle* lays out the core of Unification Church theology and is held by its believers to have the status of holy scripture." (3) (Beliefs)

C. "The Moonies interpret much of the Bible allegorically; they teach that the thieves on the cross represent democracy (the 'right') and communism (the 'left'). They claim that 'resurrection' does not refer to raising the dead, but to accepting the 'word of God.'" (2) (2. Method of Interpretation)

D. Proof texts: <u>John 17:17</u>, <u>Proverbs 30:6</u>

2. Salvation

A. "Eve was tempted by the snake, i.e., Satan, with whom she had intercourse. That caused the *spiritual fall*. Later on, she had illicit intercourse with Adam, (84) causing the *physical fall*. Therefore, a physical as well as a spiritual salvation was called for, and that is why Jesus was born...Jesus' mission did not succeed...Jesus should have married and thus instituted marriage, or salvation,... he did so in Heaven...he married the Holy Spirit and thereby guaranteed the *spiritual salvation*...However, physical salvation was not accomplished...we now need a new Messiah, the Lord of the Second Advent, who is able to constitute the triad at the physical level just as Jesus did at the spiritual level." (5) (The Doctrine of Salvation in the Unification Church)

B. "Moonies claim that marriage is the most important means of establishing God's kingdom on earth...and that only those who are married will be saved, or qualified, for the kingdom." (2) (11. Marriage)

C. "The actual wedding is combined with a holy wine ceremony where hundreds of couples drink wine mixed with Rev. Moon's own blood (sacrament-imitation), and sprinkled with water (baptism-imitation)...they are adopted into Rev. Moon's family, and they and their children will share the...sinlessness of his family." (5) (The Doctrine of Salvation in the Unification Church)

D. Proof texts: Romans 5:1, 8, 11, 15, 17, 21

3. Baptism

A. "...the Christian ordinances of baptism and communion are avoided by the Unification Church..." (2) (4. The Occult)

B. Proof Text: Matthew 3:13-17

4. The Church

A. "In order to promote the unity of (1) Christian theologies, (2) Christian denominations, and (3) Christian churches, And (4) to accomplish an inter-faith movement that Heavenly Father has given us as a great commandment before the Glorious Day of the Lord of the Second Coming takes place, to build the Kingdom of Heaven on Earth for all mankind to live in peace and order and joy forever. Amen." (6) (One World Church making heaven on earth)

B. "Marriage is central to the teachings of the church, and the wedding of Moon to Hak Ja Han in 1960...the marriage of the Lamb foretold in the book of Revelation...established the position of True Parents...the first couple...to bring forth children with no original sin...all people...can receive the blessing of God upon their marriages through the Moons...The number of couples who have received this blessing...was 360,000 by 1995." (1) (pg 329)

C. "God is now throwing Christianity away and is now establishing a new religion, and this religion is the Unification Church...All the Christians in the world are destined to be absorbed by our movement." (2) (Quotes From Moon)

D. Proof Texts: Colossians 1:17-19, Matthew 16:13-18

5. Jesus Christ

A. "According to Moon, it was God's plan for Jesus to find a perfect mate and produce sinless children, bringing about the world's physical and spiritual salvation. But Jesus failed because He couldn't get the Jews to accept him as Messiah. The Crucifixion was a 'mistake' which thwarted God's plans and made it necessary for a new Messiah to come during this present age. This new 'messiah', called the 'Lord of the Second Advent' by Moon, was born in Korea in 1920 (which coincidentally, is the place and time of his own birth)." (2) (Summary)

B. "Moonies deny the deity of Jesus...just a man, not God...not virgin born... They do not believe that Jesus was physically resurrected, but that He returned as a spirit..." (2) (7. Jesus Christ)

C. "...Jesus couldn't go to Heaven, until Moon married him to a Korean woman (in 1978) and they raised spiritual children together." (7)

D. "In 1992...Moon declared that he and his wife are the Messiah and True Parents of all humanity." (1) (pg 330)

E. Proof Text: <u>I Corinthians 15:1-4</u>

6. The Trinity (Godhead)

A. "the 'Trinity' does not consist of Father, Son, and the Holy Spirit, but of man, woman, and God." (5) (The Doctrine of Salvation in the Unification Church)

B. "Moonies teach that the Holy spirit is a 'female spirit'-the 'True Mother' and spiritual wife of Jesus." (2) (9. Holy Spirit)

C. Proof Text: <u>II Corinthians 13:14</u>

7. Heaven And Hell

A. "Moonies teach that heaven is a realm of the spirit world and that hell is inconsequential because it will 'pass away as heaven expands' and all mankind is redeemed. Also, one's destination after death depends on his spirit's 'quality of life on earth; by the degree of goodness we build into them through actions.'" (2) (13. Heaven and Hell)

B. Proof text: <u>Luke 16:22-23</u>

THIS GROUP IS DEFINITELY A FALSE DENOMINATION BASED ON A FALSE CHRIST (MOON) AND WORKS FOR SALVATION.

---

(1) <u>Handbook Of Denominations</u>, 11th Edition, Revised by Craig D. Atwood, Abington Press, Nashville, 2001.

(2) <u>Unification Church Christian or Cult?</u>, https://www.tapatalk.com/groups/- cultbustersgalactica/moonies-cult-beliefs-t1057.html

(3) <u>Unification Church</u>, http://en.wikipedia.org/wiki/Unification_Church

(4) <u>Founder's son takes on South Korea Unification Church leadership</u>, April 19, 2008

https://culteducation.com/group/1277-unification-church/23889-founders-son-takes-on-skorea-unification-church-leadership.html

(5) <u>Vital Information on the Unification Church</u>, https://web.archive.org/web/201702-25043849/http://www.caic.org.au/biblebase/moonies/moonies2.htm

(6) <u>Declaration of Unification Theological Affirmations at Barrytown, New York</u>, 1976

http://www.tparents.org/library/unification/topics/traditn/Declaration-Faith.htm

(7) <u>The Truth About Sun Myung Moon</u>,

https://freedomofmind.com/the-truth-about-sun-myung-moon/

DENOMINATIONS-Lesson 32

Unitarian Universalist Association

I Corinthians 3:18-20

Origin: "Unitarian Universalism is a liberal religious tradition that was formed from the consolidation of two religions: Unitarianism and Universalism. In America, the Universalist Church of America was founded in 1793, and the American Unitarian Association in 1825. After consolidating in 1961, these faiths became the new religion of Unitarian Universalism through the Unitarian Universalist Association (UUA)." (1) "Unitarianism: Generically, the rejection of the doctrine of the Trinity[1] in favor of the idea that God is exclusively one person...Universalism: Generically, the belief that all people will eventually receive salvation and eternal life...the UUA does not even profess to be a specifically Christian body." (2) "The beliefs of individual Unitarian Universalists range widely; Religious humanism, Judaism, Christianity, Islam, Hinduism, Sikhism, Buddhism, Taoism, Syncretism, Neopaganism, Atheism, Agnosticism, New Age, Omnism, Pantheism, Panentheism, Pandeism, Deism, and teachings of the Bahá'í Faith." (3) "We uphold the free search for truth. We will not be bound by a statement of belief. We do not ask anyone to subscribe to a creed. We say ours is a noncreedal religion. Ours is a free faith." (4) (What We Believe)

Doctrinal Beliefs:

1. The Bible

A. "We believe that personal experience, conscience and reason should be the final authorities in religion. In the end religious authority lies not in a book or person or institution, but in ourselves..." (4)

B. "the Bible...is...one among a number of divine books...The writings of Buddha, Mohammed, Confucius, Lao, and the Vedas and Upanishads are

---

1. http://www.wfial.org/index.cfm?fuseaction=archives.index&#Trinity

sources of revelation, none of which are infallible, but all...contribute something to the religious growth and development of mankind." (5) (Pg-424)

C. "We do not...hold the Bible-or any other account of human experience-to be either an infallible guide or the exclusive source of truth. Much biblical material is mythical or legendary...We believe that we should read the Bible as we read other books (or the newspaper)-with imagination and a critical eye." (6) (And about the Bible)

D. "We believe that religious wisdom is everchanging. Human understanding of life and death, the world and its mysteries, is never final. Revelation is continuous." (4)

E. Proof texts: <u>Psalms 119:98-100</u>, <u>Romans 3:3-4a</u>

2. Salvation

A. "...salvation has come to be associated with a specific set of beliefs or a spiritual transformation of a very limited type...Among Unitarian Universalists, instead of salvation you will hear of our yearning for...personal growth, increased wisdom, strength of character, and gifts of insight, understanding, inner and outer peace..." (6) (How do UUs understand salvation?)

B. "Because of the total depravity of man, supposedly, God sent His only begotten Son to the world to die for sinful men. Such doctrine Unitarians find offensive, unbiblical, even immoral. It is certainly inconsistent with the nature of God or the dignity of man..." (7)

C. "They draw from a variety of religious traditions. Individuals may or may not self-identify as Christians or subscribe to Christian beliefs." (3) (Puritan roots and Congregationalist background)

D. Proof texts: <u>Romans 5:8</u>, <u>Galatians 2:16</u>, <u>Psalms 100:3</u>

3. Baptism

A. "Many Unitarian Universalist congregations no longer observe the Christian sacraments of baptism...'Child dedications' often replace more traditional infant baptisms..." (3) (Services Of Worship)

B. "Baptism is administered to children (rarely to adults), more for sentimental reasons..." (8) (Unitarians, Name and Doctrine)

C. Proof Text: Acts 16:32-34

4. The Church

A. "Each UU congregation is autonomous—congregational leaders set their own priorities and choose their own ministers and staff. Congregations vote for the leaders of the UUA..." (1) (About The UUA)

B. "The first denominationally ordained woman minister was the Universalist Olympia Brown...she was duly ordained...in 1863." (9) (pg 40)

C. "John Buehrens, president of the 250,000-member group said, 'We teach that homosexuality is not a sin, but homophobia is a sin...'" (10)

D. "Unitarian Universalists have been in the forefront of the work to make same-sex marriages legal in their local states and provinces, as well as on the national level. Gay men, bisexuals, and lesbians are also regularly ordained as ministers, and a number of gay, bisexual, and lesbian ministers have, themselves, now become legally married to their partners. In May 2004, Arlington Street Church, in Boston, Massachusetts, was the site of the first state-sanctioned same-sex marriage in the United States." (3) (Politics of Unitarian Universalists)

E. Proof Texts: I Timothy 2:12, Romans 1:24-28

5. Jesus Christ

A. "We repudiate the doctrine of the virgin birth and do not believe Jesus is: God incarnate (in flesh), the second person of the trinity, the Messiah of Jewish hope or of Christian fantasy. Also, Jesus is not the final arbitrator at the end of time who shall judge the quick and the dead." (7)

B "Unitarianism views Jesus as a mere human being." (2)

C. "Unitarian Universalist Christians have understood Jesus as...a God-filled human being, not a supernatural being...Jesus' very human life...in line with, the great Jewish tradition of prophets and teachers." (6) (What about Jesus?)

D. Proof Text: <u>John 1:1-3, 14</u>

6. The Trinity (Godhead)

A. "In general, a Unitarian is a religious person...who believes in one God-not the Trinity." (7)

B. "The word 'God' is much abused. Far too often, the word seems to refer to a kind of granddaddy in the sky or a super magician. To avoid confusion, many Unitarian Universalists are more apt to speak of 'reverence for life'...Unitarian Universalists generally agree that the fruits of religious belief matter more than beliefs...even about God." (6) (What Do UUs Believe About God?)

C. Proof Text: <u>II Corinthians 1:21-22</u>

7. Heaven And Hell

A. "...if by heaven, you mean an abode of eternal light, where the saved and redeemed enjoy everlasting bliss, and if by hell, you mean the devil's eternal darkness, where the wicked suffer unending torment-then Unitarianism emphatically repudiates such beliefs." (7)

B. Proof texts: <u>Luke 23:43</u>, <u>Revelation 20:15</u>

THIS GROUP IS DEFINITELY A FALSE DENOMINATION WHICH DENIES THE DIVINITY OF CHRIST AND TEACHES THAT ALL WILL BE SAVED.

---

(1) <u>History Of Unitarian Universalism</u>, https://www.uua.org/beliefs/who-we-are/history

(2) <u>Index of Cults and Religions</u>, https://www.watchman.org/index-of-cults-and-religions/#U

(3) <u>Unitarian Universalism</u>, http://en.wikipedia.org/wiki/Unitarian_Universalism

(4) <u>What We Believe</u>, by Reverend Marta Flanagan, https://www.firstparish.info/ about/about-unitarian-universalism/what-we-believe/

(5) *The Kingdom of the Cults*, Walter Martin, Bethany Fellowship, Inc., Minneapolis, Minnesota, 1965, 1977

(6) <u>Our Unitarian Universalist Faith: Frequently Asked Questions</u>, By Alice Blair Wesleyhttps://www.uuabookstore.org/Assets/PDFs/3017.pdf

(7) <u>What is a Unitarian?</u>, Look Magazine, March 8, 1955 Issue. (Answers to questions submitted *by Look Magazine* were given by Rev. Carl M. Chworowsky, minister of the First Unitarian Church of Fairfield, Connecticut.)

(8) *Catholic Encyclopedia*: <u>Unitarians</u>, Volume XV. Published 1912. New York: Robert Appleton Company. http://www.newadvent.org/cathen/15154b.htm

(9) *American Universalism*, by George Huntston Williams, 4th Edition, 2002, Skinner House Books, Boston

(10) <u>Boy Scouts Rebuff Critics</u>, *The Sword of the Lord*, Murfreesboro, TN, 8/4/1998

DENOMINATIONS-Lesson 33

United Church of Christ/Congregational/ Puritan/ Pilgrim

<hr>

I **I Timothy 4:2-4**

Origin: "The Congregational Churches were organized when the Pilgrims of Plymouth Plantation (1620) and the Puritans of the Massachusetts Bay Colony (1629) acknowledged their essential unity in the Cambridge Platform of 1648...The United Church of Christ came into being in 1957 with the union of two Protestant denominations: the Evangelical and Reformed Church and the Congregational Christian Churches." (1) "The United Church of Christ (UCC) is a socially liberal mainline Protestant Christian denomination based in the United States...with approximately 4,700 churches and 745,230 members" in 2022. (2) (Introduction) "notable people known to have been past or present members or raised in the United Church of Christ...Howard Dean...Hubert Humphrey...Barack Obama... Andrew Young...Oprah Winfrey..." (2) (List of notable UCC members)

Doctrinal Beliefs:

1. The Bible

A. "*There is yet more light and truth to break forth from God's holy word.* This affirmation by one of the founders of the Congregational tradition assumes the primacy of the Bible as a source for understanding the Good News and as a foundation for all statements of faith." (1)

B. "Today, the wide interpretation of scripture, informed by the Holy Spirit and individual conscience, results in no consensus about what constitutes 'right doctrine.'" (3) (Pg 51)

C. Congregationalist and United Church of Christ writers use many modern translations in their writings (NASB, NRSV, NIV, CEV among others).

D. The New Revised Standard Version has changed hell to hades 10 times. The KJV has 84 references to "Lord Jesus Christ", NRSV has only 60!

E. Proof texts: <u>Ephesians 3:14</u>, <u>II Corinthians 2:17</u>

2. Salvation

A. "God promises to all who trust in the gospel forgiveness of sins...the presence of the Holy Spirit...and eternal life in that kingdom which has no end." (4)

B. "All shades of theological opinion have found welcome in its ranks, from Calvinistic orthodoxy to an extreme liberalism that can scarcely be distinguished from Unitarianism." (5) (pg 680) (Calvinism holds to five points; total depravity, unconditional election, limited atonement, irresistible grace and perseverance of the saints.) (The Unitarians accept ALL religions as right.)

C. Proof Texts: <u>John 3:16</u>, <u>Romans 10:9-13</u>

3. Baptism

A. "Water in adequate supply may be in the baptistry, a font, a bowl, or a pitcher, depending upon local custom...This is the water of baptism. Out of this water we rise with new life, forgiven of sin and one in Christ, members of Christ's body... Baptism is the sacrament through which we are united to Jesus Christ...The pastor, administering the water by pouring, sprinkling, or immersion...If there are no infants or young children to be baptized, continue with the questions for older children and adults" (6)

B. "Clergy and laity were invited to select two meanings of baptism...Baptism as an 'entry into the Church Universal' was the most frequent response" (2) (Studies and Surveys of Beliefs)

C. Baptism of infants or using any other mode than immersion is unscriptural.

D. Proof texts: <u>Acts 2:41</u>, <u>Mark 1:9-10</u>

4. The Church

A. "The National Association of Congregational Christian Churches formed, in part, to ensure the continuation of this core Congregational principle, local church autonomy." (3) (Pg 26)

B. "*That they may all be one.* [John 17:21] This motto of the United Church of Christ reflects the spirit of unity on which it is based and points toward future efforts to heal the divisions in the body of Christ. We are a uniting church as well as a united church." (1) (What We Believe)

C. "Approximately 50.9% of active, non-retired Authorized Ministers in the United Church of Christ identified as male, 49.0% identified as female, and 0.1% identified as transgender/gender-variant." (7) (UCC Authorized Ministers By Gender Demographics)

D. "The problem today is that many are claiming that homosexuality is not a sin ...the homosexual can serve Jesus Christ even while continuing to practice his homosexuality...an error which the United Church of Christ has promoted vigorously 1972—William Johnson became the first openly homosexual person to be ordained by a mainline denomination...1977—In Virginia, Anne Holmes became the first openly lesbian woman ordained in the UCC...1991—The UCC General Synod 'boldly affirms, celebrates and embraces the gifts of ministry of lesbian, gay and bisexual persons.'" (8) (pg 75-76)

E. Proof texts: <u>II Thessalonians 3:6</u>, <u>I Timothy 2:12</u>, <u>I Corinthians 6:9-11</u>

5. Jesus Christ

A. "In Jesus Christ, the man of Nazareth, our crucified and risen Lord, God has come to us and shared our common lot, conquering sin and death and reconciling the whole creation to its creator." (4)

B. "Because Christ is the head of the church, each local church is in a dynamic process of understanding the will and purposes of Christ for their particular ...church." (3) (Pg 66)

C. "The United Church of Christ...glories in its 'unity in diversity.' This means there is a great variety of doctrine within its midst. There are those who deny the deity of Jesus Christ and those who affirm it..." (8) (Pg 77)

D. Proof Texts: John 1:1-3, Colossians 1:16-20

6. The Trinity (Godhead)

A. "In...*Witness* magazine, Winter 1996 issue, Dr. Donald Bloesch, Professor of Theology at Dubuque Seminary and one of the most widely known and read UCC theologians, made this assessment...the UCC...sees the three persons of the trinity as metaphors rather than distinct entities." (8) (Pg 74-75)

B. "We give you thanks, O Holy One, mother and father of all the faithful..." (6) (Prayer For the Baptized)

C. "In 1996, the UCC published a politically-correct, feminized hymnal that contains hymns which address God as Mother. The lyrics to 'Be Thou My Vision', for example, were changed to read: "Mother and Father, you are both to me/ now and forever, your child I will be." (8) (pg 74)

D. Proof Text: John 14:16-17

7. Heaven And Hell

A. "United Church of Christ...Does not teach that heaven and hell are actual places in the universe. Adherents make up their own minds about the nature of heaven and hell through scriptural precedent, though most believe that heaven and hell are states of mind." (9) (Stance on Heaven)

B. Neither heaven nor hell are mentioned in the *Statement Of Faith Of The United Church Of Christ*.

C. Proof texts: John 3:36, John 5:28-29

THIS GROUP IS A FALSE DENOMINATION PRACTICING BAPTISMAL REGENERAT-ION AND WELCOMING THOSE WHO DO NOT BELIEVE IN THE DEITY OF JESUS CHRIST.

---

(1) <u>What is the United Church of Christ?</u>, https://www.ucc.org/domestic-policy/ ourfaithourvote_about/about-us_what-is-the-united-church-of/

(2) <u>United Church Of Christ</u>, http://en.wikipedia.org/wiki/United_Church_of_Christ

(3) <u>The Art And Practice Of The Congregational Way</u>, (Download)https://www.naccc. org/about-us/ about-congregationalism/

(4) <u>United Church of Christ Statement of Faith—adapted by Robert V. Moss</u>, https:// www.ucc.org/ what-we-believe/worship/statement-of-faith/#Robert-V.-Moss-Version

(5) <u>A Manual of Church History</u>, Vol. 2, Albert Henry Newman, Judson Press, Valley Forge, 1902, 1931, 1972.

(6) <u>Order For Baptism</u>, http://d3n8a8pro7vhmx.cloudfront.net/unitedchurchofchrist/legacy_url/ 1029/baptism .pdf?1418424428

(7) <u>The United Church Of Christ: A Statistical Profile, Fall 2016</u>, http://uccfiles.com/pdf/Fall-2016-UCC-Statistical-Profile.pdf

(8) <u>Protestant Denominations Today</u>, https://www.wayoflife.org/free_ebooks/ protestant_denominations_today.php

(9) <u>Christian Salvation?</u>, https://infidels.org/kiosk/article/christian-salvation-192.html

DENOMINATIONS-Lesson 34

United Pentecostal Church International (UPCI)

<hr>

Matthew 28:18-20

<hr>

ORIGIN: "The UPCI emerged out of the Pentecostal movement that began with a Bible school in Topeka, Kansas in 1901 and with the Azusa Street Revival in Los Angeles, California, in 1906. It traces its organizational roots to October 1916, when a large group of ministers withdrew from the Assemblies of God over the doctrinal issues of the oneness of God and water baptism in the name of Jesus Christ...The United Pentecostal Church Inter-national (UPCI)... was formed in 1945 by the merger of the Pentecostal Church Incorporated and the Pentecostal Assemblies of Jesus Christ. From 521 churches in 1945, the UPCI has grown to more than 43,000 churches (including preaching points), 41,000 credentialed ministers, and 5.5 million constituents worldwide. The UPCI currently has a presence in 238 nations and territories." (1)

Doctrinal Beliefs:

1. The Bible

A. "We believe the Bible to be inspired of God; the infallible Word of God...The Bible is the only God-given authority which man possesses; therefore, all doctrine, faith, hope, and all instruction for the church must be based upon, and harmonize with, the Bible." (2) (Preamble)

B. "We continue to recognize the King James Version of the Bible, because of its historic influence, as a trusted and prominent translation of the Scriptures to be used in our churches and among our people." (3)

C. Proof text: II Timothy 3:16-17

2. Salvation

A. "The basic and fundamental doctrine of this organization shall be the Bible standard of <u>full salvation</u>, which is repentance, baptism in water by immersion in the name of the Lord Jesus Christ for the remission of sins, and the baptism of the Holy Ghost with the initial sign of speaking with other tongues as the Spirit gives utterance." (2) (Fundamental Doctrine)

B. "A Christian, to keep saved, must walk with God and keep himself in the love of God...and in the grace of God. The word 'grace' means 'favor'. When a person transgresses and sins against God, he loses his favor. If he continues to commit sin and does not repent, he will eventually be lost and cast into the lake of fire." (2) (The Grace of God)

C. Proof texts: <u>Ephesians 2:8-10</u>, <u>I Peter 1:5</u>

3. Baptism

A. "The Scriptural mode of baptism is immersion, and is only for those who have fully repented, having turned from their sins and a love of the world. It should be administered by a duly authorized minister of the Gospel, in obedience to the Word of God, and in the name of our Lord Jesus Christ..." (2) (Water Baptism)

B. "Sprinkling, pouring, or infant baptism of any kind cannot be substantiated by the Word of God, but are only human traditions." (4) (Mode of Baptism)

C. "Baptism is carried out in Jesus' name only." (5) (pg 289) (Jesus Only doctrine)

D. "Water baptism is an essential part of New Testament salvation and not merely a symbolic ritual. It is part of entering into the kingdom of God (God's church, the bride of Christ)" (4) (Water Baptism)

E. Proof Text: <u>Matthew 28:19-20</u>, <u>Titus 3:5</u>

4. The Church

A. "UPCI polity is essentially congregational, with autonomous local churches. The General Conference of the church meets annually to elect officials. A general superintendent, two assistants, and a secretary-treasurer are members of a general board that also includes district superintendents, executive presbyters, and division heads." (5) (pg 289)

B. "We shall endeavor to keep the unity of the Spirit until we all come into the unity of the faith, at the same time admonishing all brethren that they shall not contend for their different views to the disunity of the body." (2) (Fundamental Doctrine)

C. Proof Text: Acts 9:31

5. Jesus Christ

A. "The one true God, Jehovah of the Old Testament, took upon Himself the form of man, and as the Son of man, was born of the virgin Mary." (2) (The Son of God)

B "It took shedding of blood for remission of the sins of the world...but God the Father was a Spirit and had no blood to shed. Thus He prepared a body of flesh and blood...and came to earth as a man in order to save us..." (4) (Son)

C. "The vicarious suffering of the Lord Jesus Christ paid for the healing of our bodies, the same as for the salvation of our souls...We see from this that divine healing for the body is in the atonement." (2) (Divine Healing)

D. "Jesus Christ is coming back to earth in bodily form, just as He went away... He will catch away a holy people (His bride, His church) who have accepted redemption through His blood, by birth of water and of the Spirit, and who are found faithful when He comes." (4) (Second Coming Of Christ)

E. Proof Texts: Luke 11:1-2, John 3:16

6. The Trinity (Godhead)

A. "We believe in the one ever-living, eternal God: infinite in power, holy in nature, attributes and purpose; and possessing absolute, indivisible deity." (2) (The One True God)

B. "The doctrinal views of the UPCI reflect most of the beliefs of the Holiness-Pentecostal movement, with the exception of...the historic doctrine of the Trinity, and the traditional trinitarian formula in water baptism" (5) (pg 289)

C. "...Father, Son, and Holy Ghost are not names of separate persons, but titles of positions held by God." (4) (Formula for Water Baptism)

D. "The Holy Ghost is not a third person in the Godhead, but rather the Spirit of God (the Creator), the Spirit of the resurrected Christ." (4) (Holy Ghost)

E. Proof Texts: <u>I John 5:7</u>, <u>II Corinthians 13:14</u>

7. Heaven And Hell

A. "The eternal destiny of every soul shall be determined by a just God who knows the secrets of everyone's heart." (4) (Judgment)

B. When the thousand years are finished, there shall be a resurrection of all the dead...summoned before the great white throne for their final judgment, and all whose names are not found written in the Book of Life shall be cast into the lake of fire, burning with brimstone which God hath prepared for the Devil and his angels, Satan himself being cast in first." (2) (Final Judgment)

C. "Jesus Christ is coming again to catch away His church. In the end will be the final resurrection and the final judgment. The righteous will inherit eternal life, and the unrighteous eternal death." (1) (Our Beliefs, About The Future)

D. roof texts: <u>Romans 10:9-10</u>, <u>Revelation 20:5-6, 11-15</u>

THIS GROUP IS A FALSE DENOMINATION WHO REJECT THE TRINITY, TEACH THAT JESUS WAS JUST GOD THE FATHER IN THE FLESH. THEY ALSO TEACH THAT SALVATION IS ONLY ACHIEVED BY REPENTANCE, BAPTISM, THE BAPTISM OF THE HOLY GHOST, SPEAKING IN TONGUES AND REMAINING FAITHFUL.

(1) About the UPCI, https://upci.org/about-the-upci/

(2) The Official Creed of the United Pentecostal Church International, UPCI, https:// www.bible.ca/cr-United-Pentecostal-(upci).htm

(3) Bible Translations, Adopted by the General Board in 2022, https://upci.org/wp-content/uploads/2023/02/Bible-Translations-Position-Paper.pdf

(4) The Apostles' Doctrine, https://apostoliconenesspentecostals.wordpress.com/statement-of-faith/

(5) Handbook Of Denominations, 11th Edition, Revised by Craig D. Atwood, Abington Press, Nashville, 2001.

DENOMINATIONS-Lesson 35

Unity School of Christianity

I **John 4:1-3**

Origin: "Unity was founded by Charles and Myrtle Fillmore in 1889, and was later incorporated as a church in 1903 by the Unity Society of Practical Christianity in Kansas City...The Fillmores were students of Phineas Parkhurst Quimby, a mental healer and metaphysician. Myrtle was also a follower of Mary Baker Eddy, the founder of Christian Science, who was likewise influenced by Quimby. Unity, therefore, was birthed by the Fillmores, but its roots go back directly to Mary Baker Eddy and both directly and indirectly to Phineas Quimby." (1) (History) In 1924 "...the Fillmores established the Unity Church Universal..." (2) (Pg 278) Today, "they are influential, with a mail order to 6 million people, with well financed radio and TV promotions...they print millions of pieces of literature, like the periodical 'Wee Wisdom', appealing to Sunday school children, and the devotional 'Daily Word', using the name of Christianity and the Bible to teach Hindu Doctrines..." (3) "...its adherents usually retain their membership in the church of their choice, while at the same time subscribing to the Unity publications, thus giving them a direct access to many churches and many congregations where the Unity cult teachings are subtly disseminated under the guise of a higher plane of Christian experience...with a reputed world member-ship of approximately 1,000,000...." (2) (Pg 275)

Doctrinal Beliefs:

1. The Bible

A. "...spiritual principle is embodied in the sacred books of the world's living religions...the Bible...other Scriptures, such as the Zend-Avesta, and the *Upanishads*, as well as the teachings of Buddha, the *Koran*, and the *Tao* of Lao-tse and the writings of Confucius, contain expressions of eminent spiritual truths..." (2) (Pg 279)

B. "We look upon the Genesis story as an allegory; a very human attempt to explain our beginnings." (4) (Genesis story allegory)

C. "...Scripture may be a satisfactory authority for those who are not themselves in direct communion with the Lord." (2) (Pg 279)

D. Charles Fillmore declared in a 1914 lecture on Bible interpretation: "I think sometimes we would get along a little faster in our understanding of the Absolute Truth if we quit this constant quotation of Scripture." (5)

E. Proof texts: Psalms 12:6-7, Matthew 19:3-6

2. Salvation

A. "Sin...defined as...'living under a false sense of separation from God.' We view this as a delusion because God is in reality continuously present within us. This false belief can be overcome through prayer." (4) (Sin)

B. "Salvation, comes by recognizing that each person is as much a Son of God as Jesus is. There is no evil, no devil, no sin, no poverty, and no old age. A person is reincarnated until he learns these truths and becomes 'perfect'... 'positive thinking' is the key to everything..." (3)

C. "Salvation is now—not something that occurs after death. It happens whenever we turn our thoughts from fear, anxiety, worry, and doubt to thoughts of love, harmony, joy, and peace." (6) (**What does Unity teach about sin and salvation, heaven and hell?**[1])

D. Proof texts: Isaiah 59:2, Romans 5:1-2

3. Baptism

A. "Within Christendom, some faith groups...totally immerse the body in water ...others...simply sprinkle drops of water on the person. Most Unity practitioners do neither. We note that Jesus never made baptism a requirement for others during his ministry; and so, we do not have a formal baptism sacrament. Rather we encourage every believer to attain Spiritual Baptism

---

1. http://www.unityonline.org/aboutunity/whoWeAre/faq.html#sin

which is a deeply personal event, a cleansing 'prayer experience with Spirit, an ultimate dialogue between an individual and God.' The individual emerges purified, having experienced a religious conversion..." (4) (Baptism)

B. "Whereas baptism by water represents the cleansing of the consciousness, spiritual baptism signifies the inflow of the Holy Spirit. Baptism is a mental and spiritual process that takes place within the individual as he or she aligns with the spirit of God". (6) (**Does Unity practice baptism and communion?**)

C. Proof Text: <u>Matthew 28:19-20</u>

4. The Church

A. "Unity's distinction is that the follower of its teaching is encouraged to remain in his respective church home whether it be Baptist, Methodist, Presbyterian, or whatever...followers of Unity consider their denominational affiliation as a mission field where they can subtly disseminate their ideas." (1) (Conclusion)

B. "Unity has no missionaries. We rely upon our teachings being spread by our readers and followers and by the literature itself." (4) (Unity Practices)

C. Unity proudly supports the LGBTQIA+ community. We believe everyone is divine and that every person shines with the light of God!" (7)

D. Proof Texts: <u>II Peter 2:1-2</u>, <u>I Corinthians 6:9-11</u>

5. Jesus Christ

A. "Unity rejects the...view that Jesus is a deity to be worshipped...we look upon Jesus as a great healer, miracle worker, and mystic who had direct access to God...his actions can be emulated by believers today." (4) (Jesus Christ)

B "Jesus had lived many times before and was in search of his own salvation. He was called the Son of David...he had been previously incarnated in David ...Jesus did not die as a sacrifice for anyone's sins, he did not rise physically, and he will never return in physical form." (3)

C. "Yes, Unity teaches that the spirit of God lived in Jesus, just as it lives in every person. Every person has the potential to express the perfection of Christ as Jesus did..." (6) (**Does Unity believe in the divinity of Jesus Christ?**[2])

D. Proof Texts: <u>John 1:1-3</u>, <u>Romans 14:9-10</u>

6. The Trinity (Godhead)

A. "We do not look upon God as a deity to be feared. One fundamental attribute of God is that God is Good...Unity follows a form of pantheism...God exists in all things...in humans, plants, animals, the earth itself, etc." (4) (Deity)

B. "Fillmore goes on to say, 'God does not love anybody or anything. God is the love in everybody and everything. God exercises none of His attributes except through the inner consciousness of the universe and man.'" (1) (God)

C. "The Fillmores...saw God as being both male and female." (1) (Conclusion)

D. "God is within each one of us; and is directly accessible. We need only to quietly turn within ourselves to contact God." (4) (Deity)

E. "The Father is Principle, the Son is that Principle revealed in the creative plan, the Holy Spirit is the executive power of both the Father and the Son, carrying out the plan." (2) (Pg 279)

F. Proof Texts: <u>Ecclesiastes 12:13-14</u>, <u>John 14:16-17</u>

7. Heaven And Hell

A. "Heaven and hell are states of consciousness, not geographical locations. We make our own heaven or hell here and now by our thoughts, words, and deeds." (6) (**What does Unity teach about sin and salvation, heaven and hell?**)

B. Proof texts: <u>John 14:1-3</u>, <u>Revelation 14:9-11</u>

THIS GROUP IS A NON-CHRISTIAN FALSE DENOMINATION, NOT BELIVING IN THE DEITY OF CHRIST, HEAVEN OR HELL, AND TEACHING SALVATION BY POSITIVE THINKING.

---

2. http://www.unityonline.org/aboutunity/whoWeAre/faq.html#divinity

(1) <u>Unity School of Christianity</u>, Russ Wise, http://www.leaderu.com/orgs/probe/docs/unity.html

(2) <u>Kingdom of the Cults</u>, Walter Martin, Bethany Fellowship, Inc, Publishers, Minneapolis, Minnesota, 1965, 1977

(3) <u>WICWIKI-Cults Of Christianity</u>, Unity School Of Christianity,http://www.wicwiki.org.uk/mediawiki/index.php/Cults_of_Christianity

(4) <u>Unity Church-Unity beliefs</u>, http://www.bible.ca/cr-Unity

(5) <u>Happy Birthday Charles Fillmore – This One's For You</u>!, https://kellyisola.com/ happy-birthday-charles-fillmore-this-ones-for-you/

(6) <u>Frequently Asked Questions About Unity</u>, https://www.unityofpanamacity.org/ faqs.html

(7) <u>LGBTQIA+ Communities</u>, https://www.unity.org/topic/lgbtqia-communities

DENOMINATIONS-Lesson 36

The Way International

John 14:6

Origin: "The Way, International founder, Victor Paul Wierwille...received a Master of Theology degree from Princeton Theological Seminary...Wierwille entered the ministry and served as pastor of...(United Church of Christ) in Van Wert, Ohio until he resigned his position to avoid dismissal. He had begun to reject much of his traditional Christian beliefs after claiming in 1942, 'God spoke to me audibly, just like I'm talking to you now. He said He would teach me the Word as it had not been known since the first century'...The Way formally began in 1967 on Wierwille's family farm in New Knoxville, Ohio...The organization built an effective missionary program and recruited heavily on college campuses and through their annual Rock of Ages gathering that functioned as a concert and conference. At its zenith, the organization is estimated to have had at least 35,000 active followers. By 1995 that number had already plummeted to about 20,000 by some estimates...Wierwille, fighting cancer, installed [L. Craig] Martindale as president in 1982...Dissidents questioned and rebelled against Martindale's leadership amidst violent turmoil and shocking controversy that has drained the active membership to less that 10,000 today." (1) (History)

Doctrinal Beliefs:

1. The Bible

A. "Wierwille teaches...'The Bible as a whole is not relevant to all people of all times.' He rejects the Old Testament and the Gospels as unnecessary. Only the rest of the New Testament is relevant for his group which he calls the 'Church of God'. The Way also teaches that the Bible is not the Word of God, but only contains the word of God." (2) (The Inspired Word)

B. "Wierwille has stated that he has produced the only 'pure and correct' interpretation of the Bible since the first century." (2) (Victor Paul Wierwille)

C. *"Wierwille believed that the New Testament was originally written in Aramaic. In 1957, he began his association with Aramaic Bible scholar George M. Lamsa, and Lamsa finished his translation of the Lamsa Bible in Wierwille's home. Lamsa and Wierwille produced the first American Aramaic grammar in 1960."* (3) (Publications)

D. Proof texts: II Timothy 3:16-17, II Peter 1:20-21

2. Salvation

A. "Rather than emphasizing salvation through faith *in* Christ, Wierwille...separated 'faith' from 'believing'...a very mechanical view of faith in Christ a mere intellectual or mental assent to biblical, historical facts. He also redefined repentance as just confession and belief. Thus, salvation does not involve repentance of sins but only doing 'the will of God'." (1) (Doctrine-Salvation)

B. "An individual receives the holy spirit when he is saved. The gift of the holy spirit has 9 parts...All of them are received by all believers, including the gift of speaking in tongues." (4) (Pg 115)

C. Proof texts: John 6:44, Luke 13:3, Acts 17:30

3. Baptism

A. *"Way followers reject water baptism, holding that it was not intended as a continuing practice after Pentecost, and that it applied only to Israel. With the coming of the greater (the practice of baptizing in holy spirit) the lesser (baptizing in water) is done away with.'"* (3) (Differences from mainstream Christianity)

B. Proof Text: Matthew 3:13-17

4. The Church

A. "The Way's hierarchy is structured like a tree with the international headquarters in Ohio, serving as the 'roots', national offices forming the 'trunks', states comprising the 'limbs', regional or area organizations serving as 'branches' and local congregations of 3 to 30 followers meeting in home study groups called 'twigs'. Individual members are the 'leaves.'" (1) (Organizational Structure)

B. 'The Way International' or the 'Way Bible Research Institute', most commonly called 'The Way', is a growing pseudo-Christian organization largely comprised of young adults. As most cults operate, the Way innocently infiltrates a fellowship. After the meeting they engage new Christians in Biblical discussions and invite them to Bible studies...But beware-they are dangerous and would love to steal sheep from the flock and create damaging divisions in a fellowship." (2) (The Way)

C. Proof Text: <u>Philippians 1:1</u>

5. Jesus Christ

A. "Wierwille believed that Jesus Christ had no preincarnate existence except in the mind of God the Father. He taught that Jesus was a perfect sinless man but he was never God. In his book, *Jesus Christ is not God*, Wierwille explained, 'In other words, I am saying that Jesus Christ is not God, but the Son of God. They are not co-eternal, without beginning or end, and co-equal. Jesus Christ was not literally with God in the beginning; neither does he have all the assets of God.'" (1) (Doctrine-Son)

B "Jesus Christ's existence began when he was conceived by God's creating the soul-life of Jesus in Mary" (4) (Pg 111)

C. "The most dangerous of all Wierwille's teachings are concerning the Trinity and the Deity of Christ. He teaches that Jesus is the Son of God, but not God the Son. 'You show me one place in the Bible where it says he is God,' Wierwille thunders..." (2) (The Deity Of Christ)

D. Proof Texts: <u>John 1:1-3</u>, <u>II Peter 2:1-2</u>

6. The Trinity (Godhead)

A. "The Way, International denies the Trinity and teaches a doctrine of God similar to the Arianism of the Jehovah's Witnesses...They correctly believe that there is only one God but wrongly conclude that God is limited to one Person.

They believe that only the Father is God, denying the deity of Christ and the third Person, the Holy Spirit." (1) (Doctrine-Trinity)

B. "Elohim, God alone, is the Creator of heaven and earth. The Way, like the Jehovah's Witnesses, categorically rejects any suggestion of Trinitarian doctrine." (4) (Pg 110)

C. "Wierwille absolutely rejects the Trinity calling such a doctrine paganism and polytheistic." (2) (The Trinity)

D. Proof Texts: II Corinthians 13:14, I John 5:7

7. Heaven And Hell

A. "Like Jehovah's Witnesses, the Way also teaches that the soul is the body's life force which is in the blood and that the dead cease to exist." (1) (Doctrine-Salvation)

B. "The Way also does not believe that the dead immediately go to heaven to be in the presence of the Lord, or unbelievers to hell... they believe that souls are not immortal, thus remaining dead until the final resurrection, which is known by some as 'soul sleep.'" (3) (Differences from mainstream Christianity)

C. "When he dies, the whole man dies. Body and soul are one, and at death body and soul enter the condition known as Soul Sleep...those who die in Christ will be resurrected immortal...while those who die in their sins will be raised at the last day to be totally annihilated. There is no eternal hell for the wicked or anyone else." (4) (Pg 27)

D. Proof texts: John 14:1-3, Revelation 14:9-11

THIS GROUP IS A FALSE DENOMINATION WITH INCORRECT DOCTRINES OF THE BIBLE, THE TRINITY, JESUS CHRIST AND SALVATION.

---

(1) The Way, International, http://www.watchman.org/profile/waypro.htm

(2) Cult of Error-The Way, https://believersweb.org/cult-of-error-the-way/

(3) <u>The Way International</u>, https://en.wikipedia.org/wiki/The_Way_International

(4) <u>What The Cults Believe</u>, by Irvine Robertson, Moody Publishers, Jan. 1991

DENOMINATIONS-Lesson 37

Worldwide Church of God (1968),

———

Church of God International (1978) (Founded by Garner Ted Armstrong after his father excommunicated him.), Philadelphia Church of God (1989), Church of the Great God (1992), Global Church of God (1992), United Church of God (1995), Living Church of God (1998), Restored Church of God (1998), Grace Communion International (2009), Church of God, a Worldwide Assoc. (2010)

<u>II Timothy 4:1-4</u>

Origin: "The Worldwide Church of God...began...under the leadership of Herbert W. Arm-strong (1892-1986)." (1) (pg 337) "In the early 1930s, Herbert Armstrong began a ministry that eventually became our denomination. He had many unusual doctrines. These he taught so enthusiastically that eventually more than 100,000 people attended weekly services. After he died in 1986, church leaders began to realize that many of his doctrines were not biblical. These doctrines were rejected, and the church is now in full agreement with the statement of faith of the National Association of Evangelicals. To reflect these doctrinal changes, in April 2009, the denomination changed its name to Grace Communion Inter-national." (2) (A Brief History of Grace Communion International) "Many members did not accept these changes...In 1995, hundreds of ministers and 12,000 members left to form a different denomination." (2) (Joseph Tkach Sr.) "...in 1997 it was accepted as a member of the National Association Of Evangelicals...Over 900 churches remain affiliated around the world..." (1) (pg 339)

Doctrinal Beliefs:

1. The Bible

A. "The Holy Scriptures are by God's grace sanctified to serve as his inspired Word and faithful witness to Jesus Christ and the gospel...As such, the Holy

Scriptures are foundational to the church and infallible in all matters of faith and salvation." (3) (The Holy Scriptures)

B. "We believe that Scripture, both the Old and the New Testament...is inspired in thought and word, infallible in the original writings..." (4)

C. "When the Hebrew and Greek are translated into English, no one English translation preserves the complete essence of God's inspired thoughts... Most people have found that they benefit from using several translations rather than relying on only one." (5) (Dealing With Different Translations)

D. Research of these groups found use of 10 different English translations.

E. Proof texts: John 5:39, Proverbs 30:6

2. Salvation

A. "The gospel is the good news of...salvation by God's grace through faith in Jesus Christ. It is the message that Christ died for our sins and has made us his own before and apart from our believing in him and has bound us to himself by his love in such a way that he will never let us go." (3) (The Gospel)

B. "We believe that all who truly repent of their sins in full surrender and willing obedience to God, faithfully accepting Jesus Christ as personal Savior, are forgiven their sins by an act of divine grace...given the gift of the Holy Spirit upon Baptism...into the body of Christ, which is the true CHURCH OF GOD." (6)

C. "Some people come to faith suddenly. Something clicks in their brain, a light goes on, and they accept Jesus as their Savior. Other people come to faith in a more gradual way, slowly realizing that they do trust in Christ and not in themselves for their salvation. Either way, the Bible describes this as a new birth." (3) (Articles, What is Salvation, A New Start)

D. Proof texts: Philippians 3:9, James 2:10

3. Baptism

A. "The sacrament of baptism proclaims that we are saved by Christ alone and not through our own repentance and faith. It is a participation in the death and resurrection of Jesus Christ...Grace Communion International baptizes by immersion." (3) (Baptism)

B. "We believe in the ordinance of water baptism by immersion following repentance. Through the laying on of hands, with prayer, the believer receives the Holy Spirit and becomes a part of the spiritual body of Jesus Christ." (4)

C. "At baptism, a Christian is begotten of God and will be born into the Family of God at the resurrection" (6)

D. Proof Texts: I Corinthians 1:14-17

4. The Church

A. "The church, the Body of Christ, consists of all who have faith in Jesus Christ." (3) (The Church)

B. "We believe in observing the New Testament Passover...the seven annual Holy Days given to...Israel...those meats that are designated 'unclean' by God in Leviticus 11 and Deuteronomy 14 are not to be eaten." (4)

C. "As pastors equip the members for works of ministry, should they be training and equipping women to pastor and to teach? The answer is yes. Many women have pastoral or shepherding skills..." (7) (Conclusion)

D. Proof Texts: Revelation 1:11, Acts 20:6-7, Colossians 2:16

5. Jesus Christ

A. "The Son of God, Jesus Christ, our Lord and Savior, was born of the virgin Mary, fully God and fully human, and is the perfect revelation of the Father and the perfect representative of humanity. He suffered and died on the cross for all human sin, was raised bodily on the third day, and ascended to heaven." (3) (Summary of Our Christian Faith)

B. "We believe that the Father raised Jesus Christ from the dead after His body lay three days and three nights in the grave..." (4)

C. Proof Texts: <u>Hebrews 13:8</u>, <u>Revelation 1:5</u>, <u>John 10:17-18</u>

6. The Trinity (Godhead)

A. "We believe in one God, eternally existing, Creator of the heavens and Earth and all that is in them...The Godhead is actually composed of two personages: the God who became the Father of Jesus Christ, and the Word who was made flesh and became God's Son...We believe the Holy Spirit is the Spirit of God and of Christ Jesus" (6)

B. "God the Father is the first Person of the triune God, of whom the Son is eternally begotten and from whom the Holy Spirit eternally proceeds through the Son." (3) (God The Father)

C. Proof Texts: <u>John 14:16-17, 26</u>, <u>Matthew 12:31</u>

7. Heaven And Hell

A. "We believe the only hope of eternal life for mortal man lies in the resurrection. At the end of the Millennium, all who have lived not knowing God will be raised to physical life and given the opportunity for salvation...We believe that there shall be a resurrection of the just and unjust...the just to eternal life as spirit beings upon Earth, the unjust to the second death in hell (Gehenna) fire in which they shall perish in eternal punishment." (6)

B. "We believe that at the return of Jesus Christ a resurrection to spirit life will take place for all who have been God's faithful servants. We believe that after Jesus Christ has ruled on this earth for 1,000 years, there will be a resurrection to physical life of the vast majority of all people who have ever lived. We believe that after these people have had an opportunity to live a physical life, if they become converted, they too will receive eternal life. We also believe that those who reject God's offer of salvation will reap eternal death." (4)

C. Proof texts: <u>Luke 16:22-23</u>, <u>II Corinthians 5:6-8</u>

THESE FALSE DENOMINATIONS ALL BELIEVE THAT THE SON AND HOLY SPIRIT PROCEED FROM THE FATHER, THAT WE

RECEIVE THE HOLY SPIRIT BY BAPTISM AND IN A SECOND CHANCE TO BE SAVED FOR THE LOST AT THE RESURRECTION.

---

(1) Handbook Of Denominations, 11th Edition, Revised by Craig D. Atwood, Abington Press, Nashville, 2001.

(2) A Short History Of Grace Communion International, https://www.gci.org/aboutus/history

(3) The GCI Statement Of Beliefs, https://www.gci.org/aboutus/beliefs

(4) Fundamental Beliefs And Constitution Of The United Church Of God, (Fundamental Beliefs), http://www.bible.ca/cr-united-church-of-god-international.htm

(5) Has The Bible Been Preserved Accurately?, https://www.ucg.org/the-good-news/has-the-bible-been-preserved-accurately

(6) Summary of the Main Doctrines of the Philadelphia Church of God, https://www.pcog.org/about/pcg-doctrines

(8) Women in Church Leadership, https://www.gci.org/church/ministry/women11

DENOMINATIONAL COMPARISON CHART

Boxes marked with an "X" indicate basic agreement with our doctrinal beliefs. Foot-notes indicate any disagreements. No "X" indicates major doctrinal differences.

Denominations marked with an "F" are False Denominations.		Bible	Salvation	Baptism	Church	Jesus Christ	Trinity	Heaven & Hell
Independent Baptist		X	X	X	X	X	X	X
Baha'i Faith	F							
Brethren	F				X(U)	X		X
Buddhist	F							
Christian & Miss. Alliance		X(T)	X(S)	X(M)	X(U)	X	X	X
Christian/Church of Christ	F	X(T)			X(U)	X		X
Christian Identity	F						X	
COJCOLDS-Mormons	F							
Episcopal/Anglican	F	X(T)						
First COC (Scientist)	F							
Hindu	F							
Jehovah's Witnesses	F							
Judaism	F							
Kabbalah	F							
Lutheran	F	X(T)					X	X
Mennonite/Amish	F	X(T)		X(M)	X(U)	X	X	X
Methodist	F	X(T)				X	X	X
Muslim	F							X
Orthodox	F					X	X	X
Pentecostal	F	X(T)	X(S)(E)	X	X(U)	X	X	X
Plymouth Brethren		X(T)	X(C)			X	X	X
Presbyterian	F	X(T)				X	X	X
Reformed	F	X(T)					X	X
Roman Catholic	F						X	
Salvation Army	F	X(T)				X	X	X
Scientology	F							
Seventh-Day Adventist	F						X	
Shinto	F							
Two By Two's	F							
Unification (Moonies)	F							
Unitarian Universalist	F							
United Church Of Christ	F							
United Pentecostal	F	X			X(U)			X
Unity School	F							
Way International	F							
Worldwide Church Of God	F	X(T)		X(S)		X		

(T) Translations not KJV	(S) Holy Spirit received after salvation	(C) Five-Point Calvinism
(U) Universal Church.	(E) No Eternal Security of the believer.	
(M) Other Modes of baptism, as sprinkling or pouring.		(Revised 12/2023)

Index Of Group Names

Christian Posse Comitatus

Christian Reformed

Christian Science

Christian Separatist

Church Of Jesus Christ, Christian

Church Of Jesus Christ Of Latter-Day Saints

Church Of Christ

Church Of England

Church of God, a Worldwide Association

Church Of God In Christ

Church Of God, International

Church of God Of Prophecy

Church Of God (Seventh Day)

Church Of Jesus Christ, Aryan Nation

Church of Scientology

Church Of The Brethren

Church Of The Creator

Church of the Great God

Confederate Hammerskins

Congregational

Cooneyites

Covenant Vision Ministry

Cumberland Presbyterian

Davidian Seventh-day Adventist

Disciples Of Christ

Dunkard Brethren

Eastern Orthodox

Episcopal

Evangelical Lutheran

First Church of Christ (Scientist)

Foursquare Gospel

Free Methodist

Free Presbyterian

Free Reformed

Full Gospel

Grace Brethren

Grace Communion International

Greek Orthodox

Global Church of God

Hindu

Identity Christians

Independent Baptist

Islam

Israel Identity

Jehovah's Witnesses

Jesus Only

Jubilee

Judaism

Kabbalah

Kingdom Identity Ministries

Kingdom Of Yahweh

Ku Klux Klan

Living Word Ministries

Living Church of God

Lost Tribes Of The House Of Israel

Lutheran Church-Missouri Synod

Mennonites

Methodist

Moonies

Mormons

Muslim

Nat'l Assoc. For The Advancement Of White People

Nazarene

Old German Baptist Brethren

Orthodox

Pentecostal Holiness

Philadelphia Church of God

Pilgrim

Plymouth Brethren

Posse Comitatus

Presbyterian

Protestant Reformed

Puritan

Racial Covenant Identity

Racial Identity

Reformed

Reorg. Church Of Jesus Christ Of Latter-Day Saints

Restored Church of God

Roman Catholic

Russian Orthodox

Sacred Name

Salvation Army

Scientology

Scriptures For America Worldwide

Seventh-Day Adventist

Seventh-Day Adventist Reform Movement

Shinto

Sons Of YHVH

Stone Kingdom Ministries

The Order

The Way Corp.

The Way International

Two By Twos

Unification Church

Unitarian Universalist Association

United Church Of Christ

United Church Of God

United Methodist

United Pentecostal

Unity School Of Christianity

Vineyard Churches

Wesleyan

White Aryan Resistance

White Separatist Banner

Wisconsin Evangelical Lutheran Synod

World Church Of The Creator

Worldwide Church Of God

Word Over The World (WOW)

Yahshua's Word

Yahweh's Children

Zen Buddhism